HOW TO STOP YOUR KIDS FROM GOING BROKE!

Your step by step guide to teach your children important money and life skills (and yourself if you need to)

HOW TO STOP YOUR KIDS FROM GOING BROKE!

Your step by step guide
to teach your children
important money and life skills
(and yourself if you need to)

Sylvia Bowden

Silbo Systems
Money Lessons For Life

For help or information, please email info@silbo.co.nz

This book has been written as an educational guide. The author has taken all reasonable steps in the preparation of this book and believes the facts presented to be accurate at the time of printing. However, neither the author nor the publisher assumes any responsibility for any errors or omissions. The author and publisher specifically disclaim any liability resulting from the use or application of the information contained in this book and the information is not intended as legal advice related to individual situations.

Cover design by Martian design
Back page by John Bowden

First Edition January 2009

Kale Print. Tauranga. New Zealand

Silbo Systems

ISBN 978-0-473-14310-7

Author Sylvia Bowden

Published by Silbo Systems Ltd
PO Box 6144
Tauranga
New Zealand
info@silbo.co.nz
www.silbo.co.nz

Why should you read this book?

How to stop your kids from going broke is a must read for all parents and families. Why? 43% of people aged 18-24 spend more than they earn *(sourced from New Zealand Dept of Statistics May 2008)*.

In the twenty-first century, more than ever before, kids need to know about money. They have to be better money managers than their parents' generation to survive. Convincing advertising and a lack of financial understanding is creating debt and financial hardship in a much younger group than ever before.

Children need to know how money works at an early age so they can make informed financial choices as they grow older. The best person to teach your child about money is you! 'How to Stop Your Kids From Going Broke' provides the resources for you to impart the most valuable lessons of money and financial understanding that will ensure your children become and stay financially well. By following each step of the Silbo System your child will move from childhood to adulthood responsible for their own financial independence.

The Silbo System has been designed with eight key steps for you to learn and in turn teach your children the skills and joy of financial understanding and independence.

Read this book now – impart the lessons upon your children – they will thank you for it!

Sandra – parent of three children

As a parent I would recommend these finance lessons to every person (child or adult). We learned so many practical and different things about saving, spending and sharing. It is too much to explain. So just do these lessons and you will find it out for yourself. It brings you freedom and peace. Well done. Great course. Every home should learn these 'easy to apply' principles.

Job – 10 years old

I learned lots about money and how the bank makes their money......

Sanne – 12 years old

It is going to be absolutely awesome for when I'm older and even now. I know how to use my money wisely and not to spend it on things I don't need. I've really noticed the difference between a want and a need. I look at the world in a different perspective and see certain things differently. For example when mum goes to the bank I suddenly realise what she is doing and talking about. I understand why money is such a big thing in this world. When I am older I will look back to the money lessons and remind myself of what I have learned.

To every person who wants to positively influence the financial future of their family, friends and generations to come.

Acknowledgements

Parents are our greatest teachers in life either in a positive or negative way. I am very thankful for the skills my parents taught me while I was growing up.

Thank you Mum for giving me a monthly allowance while I was still at high school so I could learn how to manage my money and make some mistakes in a safe environment. Thank you for not rescuing me when I spent most of my first allowance on lollies and learned that it was my responsibility if I was broke. A lesson I did not appreciate at the time! Thank you for teaching me the difference between wants and needs.

Thank you Dad for teaching me valuable lessons such as reading everything before you sign it, to be honest in business dealings and to live as a person of integrity. Thank you for teaching me money was something that could be enjoyed, and giving to others could also be enjoyable. Thank you for teaching me that I didn't always have to "go with the crowd" and for passing on to me your entrepreneurial spirit.

To my parents-in-law, Arnold and Iris. Thank you for teaching your son sensible money and life skills so together we have been able to pass them on to our children.

To Pammy, Diana and Abbey. Thank you for your special friendship and encouragement. Wendy, thank you for your friendship, honest opinions and practical help.

To Elisabeth Donati, thank you for your inspirational teaching.

To my previous students, clients, and friends who were not taught money and life skills as children. Thank you for awakening in me a passion to help parents pass on "money lessons for life™" to their children so they don't end up broke.

Thank you Boyce and Barbara Haines for your godly wisdom when I first contemplated developing the Silbo System and writing this book. "Any enterprise that is built by wise planning, becomes strong through common sense, and profits wonderfully by keeping abreast of the facts" from Proverbs 24 in the bible, has helped keep me on track.

To my knight in shining armour John, my husband of 24 years, my best friend, lover, encourager and father of our two wonderful children Russell and Heather. I am thankful every single day that I am married to you. I could not have written this book without your continued encouragement and practical help.

"If you get your attitude towards money straight, it will help you straighten out almost every other area of your life."

Adapted from a quote from Billy Graham

You cannot change your past
but you can design your future.

If you are inclined to beat up on yourself for lost opportunities and bad financial decisions -

REMEMBER

yesterday is history
tomorrow is a mystery

today is a gift - that's why it's called the **present.**

A word of caution!

Sometimes we teach best what we need to learn ourselves

- **What you did in the past is done.**
- **Use it as a lesson and not an excuse.**
- **Don't let mistakes of the past become habits for the future.**

NOTE: Where possible we have chosen to use the word "he", simply to make the book consistent and easy to read. We have also used the term "parents/adult' as a generic term – it could be mum, dad, an aunt, caregiver, teacher or the person who ever reads this for themselves or works through it with a child.

Table of Contents

OUR MISSION:

Silbo Systems is dedicated to teaching you money and life skills which will empower you and your family to be and stay financially well.

Why have a system?

A system is simply a method or set of procedures for achieving or learning something.

The Silbo System has been designed in the following steps so you can learn and teach your child how to become and stay financially well.

What is the *Silbo* System?

Step One	**INTRODUCTION**	**Why have money lessons?**
Step Two	**TRANSFORM**	**Transform your thinking**
Step Three	**THINK**	**Think of others first**
Step Four	**TOIL**	**Work for what you want**
Step Five	**TRACK**	**Track where your money goes instead of wondering where it has gone**
Step Six	**TARGET**	**Have a goal to reach**
Step Seven	**TRIM**	**Trim your expenses**
Step Eight	**TRAIN**	**Train yourself how money works**

Introduction

How can you stop your kids from going broke?

First let me encourage you. Being broke won't last forever, being poor is a state of mind.

I want to tell you some of the reasons people go broke and what I have learned being a trained counsellor, life coach, budget advisor and mother of two financially responsible young adults. The word broke to me means financially sick – stressed about money – money in control of you instead of you controlling it. It may mean something else to you.

After completing a Diploma in Counselling, I was employed as a Life Coach with a community organisation. The coaching I did was conducted in the students' homes over a 12 month period. One of the five areas my students looked at as part of the course was finance. What I noticed was that it wasn't necessarily the amount of money that was coming into a home which led people to be in debt and stressed. Some people managed quite well on a low income whereas some people who were earning large incomes had just as much debt and were just as stressed as those on lower incomes. Many times the bigger the salary, the bigger the debt, the bigger the stress. Approximately 90% of my students' financial dreams/goals were simply to be debt free.

I noticed that people lacked basic financial literacy skills (how money works). My students did not understand compound interest for example and had no idea of the real cost and long term effects of borrowing money for stuff such as a car, stereo and TV which depreciated as soon as they were bought.

I was told many sad stories, especially to do with cars. Many people naively thought when they were given a loan for a car, that they must be able to make the repayments otherwise they would not have been given the loan. One couple were unable to meet the repayments of their car so it was repossessed. The car was sold for $2,000 by the finance company which left a debt of $8,000 still to be paid. So now they had no car but still $8,000 to pay and were being hounded by debt collectors.

When my job as a Life Coach was made redundant I wanted to help people with their finances so I became a budget advisor. Notice I didn't say I was made redundant like many people do. My job was made redundant, not me!

Being a budget advisor opened my eyes to the world of people in a mess financially and this is what fuelled my passion to be able to do something about it. My clients would share their lives with me at a very intimate level. Many people had made poor choices from a lack of knowledge. I met women who had moved in with their boyfriend. They agreed to take a loan in their own names or go guarantor for something that their boyfriend wanted such as a stereo or computer. When their boyfriend moved out after an argument they were often stuck paying for something that they didn't want in the first place. One way you can stop your kids and yourselves from going broke is not to go guarantor for anyone.

Relationships can breakdown in families due to financial pressures and misunderstanding about money due to different belief systems people hold about money. The book "The Four Laws of Debt Free Prosperity" indicates that money pressures contribute to 89% of all divorces and relationship breakdowns. From my experience I think that is a true statistic.

Through experience I have found that no matter how much time I spent with some people trying to help them to manage their money and get out of debt, they just seemed to go round and round in circles. This is because they had ingrained beliefs at a subconscious level about money or people with or without a lot of money. This discovery has tied in with my counselling training. Once you understand how beliefs work in your life and the lives of others you love, you can understand why you do what you do and why others do what they do with regards to money.

In lesson two – Transform your thinking - we go into how beliefs are formed about money and everything else in your life and how those beliefs show up in your everyday life.

Another thing I noticed is that people were being deceived. Advertisements for encouraging you and your children to take on consumer debt (items which depreciate as soon as they are bought) convey the feeling that you are making the right decision to buy now and pay later.

Nothing could be further from the truth because debt can cause you to worry, have health problems, cause relationship problems, and for some people commit crime. Consumer debt can cause you to become a modern day slave, a slave to your lender.

Consumer debt should be conveyed that when you take it on, all of a sudden you will realize you are in a swamp full of debt leeches who are sucking the financial life blood out of you and your family.

These leeches also seem to have the ability to crawl from one generation to another after they have finished sucking the life blood from you. They need to find new fresh blood – so they crawl and latch on to your children, and grandchildren. Unless you take action and kill those blood suckers once and for all your short term gain will turn into a long time pain.

Don't get me wrong, all debt isn't bad. There is such a thing as 'smart debt' and 'dumb debt'.

Access to easy credit has caused this generation's understanding of "needs" and "wants" to be confused.

I have been working with friends and clients and once they uncover myths and beliefs they have about money they start making huge progress in unravelling their financial mess. It doesn't happen overnight – but it does happen.

Why teach your children about money?

The answer is because 43% of people aged 18 – 24 in New Zealand have a negative net worth (are broke) and are going to be starting their life off in debt. In other words they are spending more than they are earning. Did you know that New Zealanders are spending $1.14 for every dollar they are earning? (Sourced from the New Zealand Department of Statistics in May 2008). I suspect that from what I see on the television news that this statistic would be about right for most developed countries.

What is different about this book?

In a nutshell – it addresses the "How to" for parents wanting their children to learn about money so they don't grow up broke.

As a parent you will most probably be in two categories. Either in a mess yourself financially so you think you are not qualified to teach your child about money. Or you manage your finances efficiently but don't quite know how to pass those skills on to your child. This book will empower you as a parent no matter which category you are in.

Without a doubt discussing family financial affairs is a subject that many parents shy away from and could be in the same class as discussing sex, discussed only when absolutely necessary (and generally too late)! In order to help put your child on the right financial path it is therefore vital that you (the adult) "build a bridge and get over it" and include your child in the financial life of your family. Sometimes the best way to teach your child is when they think they are not learning.

There is a misconception that schools are responsible for teaching your child to be financially intelligent. The best person to teach your child about money is you the parent. Children need to learn how money works at an early age so they can make informed choices as they grow older. You are the most important role model in your child's life. Think about what sort of a role model you are. So, what happens if your parents didn't teach you about money, or you realise you haven't handled what money you have had very well? Don't despair. What you did in the past is done. Use it as a lesson and not an excuse. Make some changes and don't let mistakes of the past become habits of the future for your next generation.

How to use

this step by step book

This book has been designed to help parents who have limited or great financial literacy skills, to be able to teach your children how money works.

We want your children to be taught to be financially intelligent by you early in life so they move from childhood into adulthood realising that they are responsible for their own financial independence. **They will thank you for it when they are grown up and have their own children.**

This step by step guide book is designed in the following format.

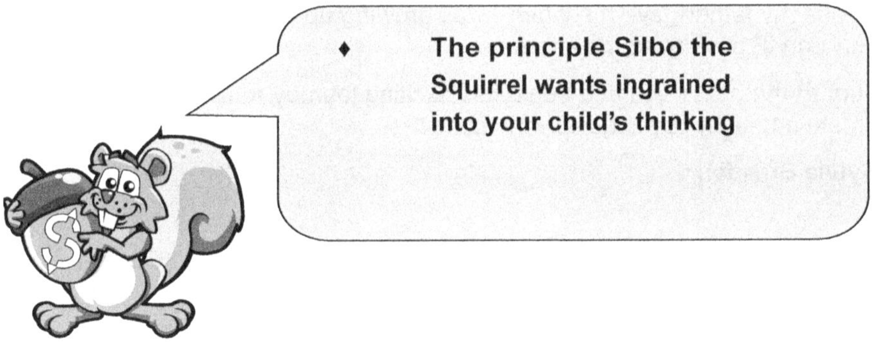

Then follows an explanation of why Silbo wants you and your child to learn this particular lesson. The idea behind using Silbo the Squirrel as the teacher, is if things get a little heated because of changes you want to make, you can say "Silbo says". We don't mind if your children get cross at Silbo instead of you. We suggest you read through all the Silbo sayings to give yourself an overview of what each lesson contains.

How to teach your child this important lesson

This is the step by step **"how to"** teach what "Silbo says".

It provides questions to ask and activities to do which will provide a basis for informing your children how to become financially intelligent.

If you read through each lesson yourself, and you don't get around to sitting down with your child and actually completing the book – don't worry. You know your child best, a lot can be learned by asking questions at the dinner table or in the car. Sometimes the best way for a child to learn is when they think they are not learning. Some children love reading and writing whereas some children will run a mile as soon they think they have to fill in a book. You just need to tap into what makes your child "tick" and find the best learning style for him or her.

Please get some professional help if you are struggling with debt. In New Zealand The Federation of Family Budgeting Services provides help at no cost to you in a practical way. Other countries will have similar services.

Take your child with you if it is possible. They will learn a lot.

For a list of services in New Zealand go to the following website *www.familybudgeting.org.nz* or consult your local telephone book.

I am happiest when I find out that what I teach makes a positive difference in someone's life. Please email me and tell me any stories of how this teaching has influenced you or your family's life

If you would like to subscribe to a regular newsletter write to *info@silbo.co.nz*

We begin step one of the Silbo System talking about contracts. The simple bit of advice my father gave me when I was growing up of "read anything fully before you sign it" has saved me a fortune!

Turn to the next page and begin this exciting journey to help you and your child create a healthy relationship with money.

Sylvia Bowden

"If you would be wealthy, think of saving as well as getting."
Benjamin Franklin

Step 1

Why Learn about money?

> "But it's not just learning things that's important. It's learning what to do with what you learn and learning why you learn things at all that matters." <u>Norton Juster</u>

Silbo says

- **Read any document fully before you sign it**
- **Find out what the consequences are if you don't keep to a contract**

Many adults sign contracts without fully understanding them or reading them thoroughly. It's important when you are asked to sign a contract that you take the time to read it and know exactly what you are signing. Many times people are told "just sign here" only to find out later that if they had read it and understood it fully they would not have signed it.

Children are sponges. If they are with you when you have signed a contract without reading it, think about what your child has just learned by what you have done. They have just learned without you saying a word, to sign a contract without reading it. When they grow up they will most times model what you did - sign a contract without reading it!

How to teach your child this important lesson

A good way to teach a child about contracts is to make a simple written agreement with your child and have them sign and date it if they agree to what is in it. You could have some fun and make up an agreement which includes a clause – I agree to wash and dry the dishes by myself for three weeks. Say "just sign here" trust me! I wouldn't get you to sign your name to something that wasn't ok. If your child didn't read it first then the best Money Lesson for Life could be to enforce the contract that your child just signed and dated. If they read it properly they will probably object to the clause about the dishes. Talk about what might have happened if your child had signed this without reading it properly.

Explain to them that when you ask for your power to be connected with a particular company then you are entering into a contract with the power company to supply you power in return for you paying the bill. The penalties for not keeping to the contract could be that your power is cut or you incur a fee for not paying your bill on time.

I was very fortunate when I was growing up that my Dad told me "never sign an agreement without reading it fully and always get a copy of what you have signed". This simple piece of advice has stuck in my head and has prevented me from making bad financial decisions from lack of knowledge of what I was signing. So to help your kids from making poor financial decisions pass on this simple bit of advice. Read any document fully before you sign it and if you don't understand it – don't sign it.

With your child, draw up a contract about how much you intend to study the Silbo System to learn about money. Agree about such things as how much time you will spend each week or day learning as much as you can about money. After you and your child have completed writing the contract, date it and sign it.

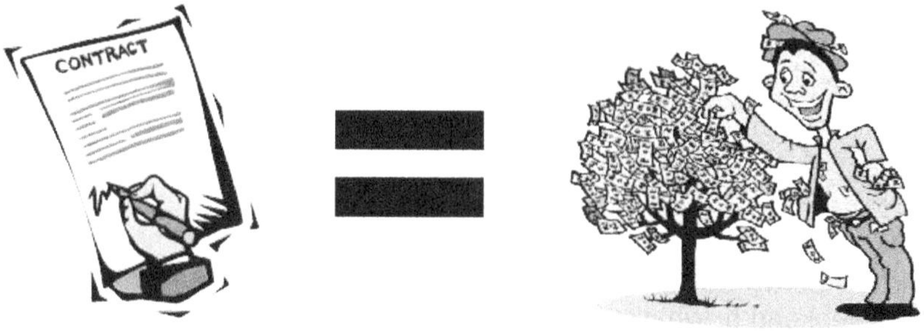

Silbo Systems Sample Contract

If you are ready to learn how money works – then sign below (once you have read and agreed to the conditions of the contract.)

I, ______________________________ (child's name), agree to the following:

I agree to discuss the Silbo System with anyone who is interested in learning about money.

I will take full responsibility for learning the Silbo System and making it part of my life.

I agree to wash, and dry the dishes by myself every night for a month.

In exchange for you agreeing to the above, Silbo Systems promises to teach you everything you need to know to help you become financially well.

Signed__________________________ Date ______________

Don't be pressured into signing anything you don't understand

Read what you sign BEFORE you sign it.

Do some research on the internet or at the library and look at what "contract" means and at the different types of contracts. Discuss who would write them up (lawyers) and what the cost might be.

More sample contracts can be found at the following website:
www.parentsinc.org.nz/family-contracts

- **People learn and remember only what they need to**
- **To be financially successful, you need to learn how money works**

In order for your child to want to learn about money, they have to see it as somehow relevant to their lives right now. Trying to get your child to think past the next weekend or what's coming up for dinner can be a difficult task let alone thinking about the next 10 or 20 or 30 years. They generally just don't want to go down that path. But if you want your child to learn the value of money and how it can help them grow up to be free of money worries, then you need to help relate it to their present lives and how it will affect their future. Find ways to relate the Silbo System to your child's passions and their own dreams and goals.

How to teach your child this important lesson

Below are some questions about money. Have your child think about money and what he knows about it now. Simply ask him the questions and let him tell you his thoughts.

Have your child close his eyes and imagine what it is like to be an older version of himself. Ask your child what he "sees" in the future. What does your child need to do to provide for himself in the future?

Discuss these questions

What would you like to learn about money?

Why do you think it would be helpful to learn about money now?

What sort of things can you get without money?

Do you think you could live without money?

Do you have to be a certain age to learn about money?

What is the best age to learn about money?

- **Follow the Silbo principles of how to stay financially well**
- **The spoken word is very powerful**

The Silbo System principles are simply the principles to follow to be and stay financially well. It's important to know the system and then participate fully to achieve financial wellness.

Unless you know what to do, and how to do it, it is very hard to stay financially well. Many adults do not know what to do to stay financially well.

How to teach your child this important lesson

You and your child should stand up and say the principles out loud. By reading them, then speaking them out loud it means you are being actively engaged in learning. You read it, speak it, then you hear what you have said, which reinforces what you have just said.

If you or your child don't know any of the words, look them up in the dictionary. You could have some fun by taking turns or seeing who could say them the softest or the loudest. You could draw squares with chalk outside and number them 1 – 25. Write in the principle and then jump into each square saying the principle out loud.

THE SILBO PRINCIPLES TO STAY FINANCIALLY WELL

- It's not chance but ***choice*** that determines my financial future
- My ***beliefs*** about money influence how I handle it
- It is ***my*** responsibility to stay financially well
- Being ***broke*** won't last forever, being ***poor*** is a state of mind
- Give away a portion of your income to ***help others***
- Find what you love to do and do it with ***passion*** and ***excellence***
- ***Save 10%*** of what you earn before you do anything
- ***Grow your money*** by putting it to work
- Making more money isn't always the answer. It's ***what I do*** with what I earn that matters
- Have written ***goals*** and ***review*** them regularly
- Interest is only ***good*** when I am ***getting*** it
- Save up for things so you can pay ***cash***
- ***Avoid*** hire purchases and personal loans
- Assets keep me ***financially well,*** liabilities keep me financially sick
- Do not borrow money for things that ***lose value***
- ***Tell*** your money where to go instead of wondering where it's gone
- Healthy money ***habits*** will put me on the path to ***financial freedom***
- ***Stick*** to a sharing, spending and savings plan
- When I ***borrow*** money I become a slave to my lender
- Being ***financially well*** will give me more choices
- ***Spend less*** than you earn by trimming expenses
- Don't put all the ***fruits*** of your labour into one basket

- Let your ***emotions*** subside then decide ***before*** spending your money
- Borrowing money for things that go down in value is ***dumb debt***
- Borrowing money for things that can go up in value is ***smart debt***

- **It is best to have open communication with your children about money**
- **Money is a tool that you can use to create financial freedom**

Setting a good example with your money habits along with good open communication, is the best way to start your children on the path to learning about money. This lesson will start the communication process and get the whole family thinking about the financial decision making in your household.

Money problems can put a huge strain on a couple's relationship and can often lead to the divorce courts. Good communication about money from an early age can help your child in his or her adult life to be open about money and able to discuss the issues and challenges that they face.

It is important that you can discuss with your child the many financial challenges that are out there in the wide world. The ability to be open with your child about your money situation may be a challenge to you but in the long run it will give them a better understanding of your financial situation. It will help make them aware of what you learned growing up or perhaps what you wished you had learned when you were younger.

How to teach your child this important lesson

You may find some of these questions a bit hard to answer if you are not used to discussing your finances with your children. However, allow them to ask you the following questions and see if you can give them an insight into your financial thinking. You may have to answer "I don't have a clue where all my money goes". The sooner you and your child start thinking about these questions and making positive changes the sooner you will reap the rewards from healthy money habits.

The idea of discussing your financial situation is so that together you can see how money is a tool and a seed and to learn how it can grow (or die) depending on how you treat it.

As you discuss your financial situation with your child, it is important to caution him about sharing your information with others. He may find himself among other children who have different financial circumstance (either better or worse) and divulging your information may cause embarrassment or shame.

Have your child interview you with these questions.

Who taught you about managing your money?

How do you track where your money goes?

What does 'financial freedom' or 'financial wellness' mean to you?

What have you done about providing for your retirement?

What was the worst investment you made?

What was the best investment you made?

What would you do differently if you could start again financially?

What else can you tell me about how you manage your money?

> "There are three realms of knowledge.
> What you know.
> What you know you don't know.
> What you don't know you don't know."
> Author unknown.

- **Ask people who are successful money managers for advice**
- **Lack of knowledge can trip you up**

This lesson is to get you and your child to think about who is the best person to ask to find out correct information.

Many people, because of the lack of knowledge of how money works, ask the wrong people for specific advice. They may ask them because they are friends or feel comfortable with them, not because they have good money skills. Time and time again when I was doing budgeting advice I would see the results of when people had asked their friends who had bad credit ratings about buying a car. My client and his friend went together to buy a car and my client ended up with a loan at 29.75% the same as his friend, all because he asked the wrong person for advice. My client ended up paying approximately $10,000 for a $5,000 car. To make matters worse, if he tried to sell this car after three years it would be worth about $3,000. This means $7,000 ($2,333 per year or $44.87 per week) of what they have paid towards the car, has been for nothing. This scenario could have been avoided if my client had sought advice from a person with good money management skills such as a budget advisor.

How to teach your child this important lesson

Go through the list and get your child to circle who they think would be the best person to ask to find out information they need. Ask him what could happen if he got poor advice or if he got advice from someone who has a lot to gain from the purchase.

Tell this true story of a previous client of mine who asked their mate how to buy a car. The car broke down less than a year after buying it. They had no money to fix it so they decided to stop paying the payments. This resulted in the car being repossessed and sold for $2,000. The debt outstanding of $8,000 was still owed and now they had no car. They then had a bad credit rating which made it difficult to borrow for a home. When you get a bad credit rating then future borrowing could be at a higher interest rate because you are more of a risk to the lender.

You can explore your own credit rating by going to the following website - www.mycreditfile.co.nz.

Who would be the best person to ask for advice?

	A	or	B
Fix the lawnmower	gardener	or	mower mechanic
Fix a leaky tap	plumber	or	builder
Fix a sore tooth	doctor	or	dentist
Build a house	builder	or	secretary
Fly an aeroplane	helicopter pilot	or	aeroplane pilot
Buy a house	tenant	or	landlord
Buy an investment	financial advisor	or	jockey
Subdivide a property	truck driver	or	surveyor
Chop down a tree	hairdresser	or	arborist
Write up a will	lawyer	or	your best friend
Buy some shares	successful investor	or	silly investor
Open a bank account	Shop assistant	or	bank officer
Plan an overseas holiday	travel agent	or	insurance agent
Buy a car	car salesperson	or	mechanic
Do a heart transplant	heart surgeon	or	brain surgeon

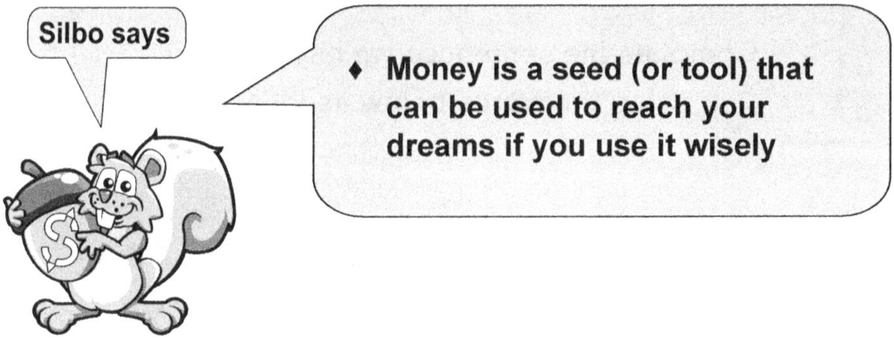

The words money, value, wealth and rich, mean something different to everyone. The idea of this lesson is for you to instil in your child that money is a tool and a means to achieving financial freedom.

Because we all have a slightly different idea of what these words mean, it is good for you to explore them with your child and look at the many ways they can be interpreted.

The term "value" is relative. The economic value of something is relative to how much the desired object is worth relative to other objects or conditions and as to how much a person wants it. Someone may value something more than another person and that is quite normal and okay.

The term "wealth" is also relative as a person on the poverty line in New Zealand or America could be classed as extremely rich in other parts of the world. For example someone who lives in Thailand and who owns their own home and has running water and electricity could be considered very rich. However, in New Zealand that would be considered "normal". Wealth can relate to having a lot of friends or money or objects or even knowledge. It can often mean that you have a lot of whatever it is.

The term "rich" is to have an abundance of whatever wealth you may have. For example: to have an amount of money or objects could be said to have a measure of wealth, but to have an abundance of money or objects could be said to be rich.

How to teach your child this important lesson

Go through the following exercise with your child and help him finish the sentences. Look up the definitions of the words on the internet or dictionary to see the many different meanings.

In the second step "Transform your thinking" we will investigate what you and your child's beliefs are about money to ascertain if those beliefs help or hinder you to be and stay financially well. If you have a belief such as "rich people are greedy and awful" then it is unlikely that you will become rich because subconsciously you don't want to be "greedy and awful".

Have a look at different foreign currency rates and see how much our money is worth in another country. Most banks have foreign currency displayed in their window or a "foreign currency" link on their websites where you can look up and see what your currency is worth compared to other currencies.

Complete the sentences we have started, using the words below as ideas.

Money means____________________________

Value means____________________________

Wealth means____________________________

Rich means____________________________

*Lots of Money *Lots of Friends

*Something that's important to me

*Gold *Owning a Yacht

*Owning a house

*A Piece of Paper *Can buy things *Cheap

*Own lots of houses *Having lots of holidays

* Financially Free *An abundance

*A Tool *Can help people *Not important

*Silly *Worth a lot *Knowledge

*Being generous *Coins *No Debt

*Having more than enough

GREEDY

Having enough to share

Nothing

Satisfaction

Silbo says

- **Many people think "life happens" to them instead of believing they can design the lives they want by making good choices**
- **Being broke is temporary, being poor is a state of mind**

You are the one that decides if you are going to be financially well or financially sick. Even though you may be experiencing hard times financially, it will pass if you make a decision to do something about it. Many people who are very wealthy now have gone through hard times and perhaps even gone bankrupt. When they are "broke" they don't see themselves as poor. They decide to learn from their mistakes and start over again. They use their past mistakes as a lesson for the future and not an excuse.

Many adults, when they think back to when they were younger, cannot remember having made a choice to be financially free when they grew up. Their main thoughts were getting a house, a car, kids, some "stuff" and having a good time.

Some people believe if they were meant to be prosperous, then they would be. There isn't anything they can do about it. Its all down to a "lucky break". However, we all have the ability to choose – to make things better than they are now or become bitter about how they are. You can choose to have a "victim" or a "survivor" mentality. A "victim" mentality is one of "it is always someone else's fault – my parents didn't train me properly" etc. A "survivor" mentality is the opposite. They think "my parents didn't train me properly, but that's okay I'm going to learn all I can so I can teach my children not to end up broke."

Your child is in a fortunate position where you are able to show him that he has a choice to have money lessons now and follow the steps needed to live a financially well life instead of one that is financially sick.

How to teach your child this important lesson

Go through the true and false questions and reinforce the principle that we all have choices to make. Discuss with your child what some of the questions and sayings might mean. For example – "I have a choice to design my financial future" means that I have a choice to make good spending decisions or poor spending decisions. Explain to your child that when he doesn't make a conscious decision to spend less than he earns, he is more likely to spend more than he earns and end up financially sick instead of financially well.

Even if you have made some poor choices in the past it is never too late to learn how money works! By learning some new skills now, you can pass those on to people that you care about so that they will become financial thrivers instead of financial survivors.

Ask your child what they think about these sayings.

I have a choice to design my financial future.	True/False
I can choose to be a smart money manager.	True/False
I can choose to control my money .	True/False
I can choose to be a financial victim or a financial survivor.	True/False
I can choose to change my financial situation.	True/False
It's not chance but choice that determines my financial future.	True/False
The power of choosing financial wellness is within reach of all of us.	True/False
Money is like a friend, if you don't treat it right, it'll go away.	True/False
There is no such thing as having no choice.	True/False
You can't make poor financial decisions today and expect to be rich tomorrow.	True/False

At dinnertime, my mother gave me two choices, take it or leave it.

- **Before you know it you will be all grown up**
- **Start thinking about the future and what you want**

Growing up seems to come round a lot quicker than we think. As we go through life there are many "firsts". Many of these firsts are age related and can be a significant moment in your child's life. This lesson is to give your child the opportunity to see what is coming up and to think about how they can be ready.

Being prepared for an event or situation gives you an advantage and can make life a whole lot easier. When you prepare for the future, you are taking control of your destiny and influencing the way your life could turn out. Being aware of what some of life's events are and at an approximate age of when you might experience them, will prepare your child for what is yet to come.

It may also help you as a parent to realise how special your children are and how quickly they grow up. It is important to train them up when they are young in the way you want them to go or not go with regards to money.

How to teach your child this important lesson

As you and you child go through the list of life's events, discuss your child's views on them and discuss how they relate to your own life experiences. Talk about events in your life such as what you or their grandparents had to do to get a drivers licence, and how it differs now.

As an exercise you could go through your child's life as they were growing up and find some important life events that have impacted them so far. Get your child to put them into some of the age squares.

The years fly by!

Have your child go through the list and put an event in a column where you think it fits. It may go in more than one column.

Ages 8-15	Ages 16-29	Ages 30-55	Ages 56 up

Life Events

Getting my driver's licence	Getting my first job	My first investment
My first savings account	Getting married	Having health problems
Buying my first car	Getting my first credit card	My parents' having health problems
Going to my high school ball	Having children	When my parents' retire
Having my first bank account	Saving for my own child's tertiary study	When I retire
Flatting for the first time	When I buy my first home	My first million dollars
When I can vote	My first overseas trip	Starting my first business
Finish school	Career change	Getting a Passport

Fill in the missing words to help you learn The Silbo Principles.

- It's not chance but __________ that determines my financial future
- My _________ about money influence how I handle it
- It is _______ responsibility to stay financially well
- Being _________ won't last forever, being _________ is a state of mind
- Give away a portion of your income to _______ ___________
- Find what you love to do and do it with ___________ and ____________
- Save ______ of __________ you ________before you do anything
- Work with ______________for what you want
- Grow _________ ____________ by putting it to work
- Making more money isn't always the answer. It's _____ I ____ with what I earn that matters
- Have written ___________ and __________ them regularly
- Interest is only ____________________ when I am _______________ it
- Save up for things so you can pay ______
- ___________hire purchases, and personal loans
- Assets keep me _______ _______, liabilities keep me________ ______
- Do _______ ____________ for things that lose value
- Tell ______ _________ where to go instead of wondering where it has gone
- Healthy money _______ will put me on the path to _______ _________
- Stick to a __________ ________________ and ____________ plan
- When I ___________ money I become a __________ to my lender
- Being ___________________ _________ will give me more choices
- _______________ ___________ than I earn by trimming expenses
- Don't put all the _____________ of your labour into one basket
- Let your _______________ subside, then decide, ____________ spending your money
- Do ______ _________ money for things that _________value
- Borrowing for things that go down in value is __________debt
- Borrowing for things that can go up in value is _________debt

(see beginning of chapter for the list of Silbo principles to stay financially well)

Fill in the blanks to help you learn the Silbo System

Introduction	Why have money lessons?
T _ _ _ _ _ F _ _M	Transform your thinking
T _ _ N K	Think of others first
T _ _ L	Work for what you want
T _ _ C _	Track where your money goes instead of wondering where it has gone
T _ R _ _ _	Have a goal to reach
T _ _M	Trim your expenses
T _ A I _	Train yourself how money works

Step 2

"Don't become so well-adjusted to your culture that you fit into it without even thinking."
<u>The message bible translation</u>

- **Your belief system about money influences how you handle it**
- **Your beliefs about money have developed in four ways**

What you believe about money will determine how it will enter and leave your life. This lesson is to help you and your child start to identify some of your beliefs and explore where they may have come from.

Our thoughts are controlled by the belief systems (about money and everything else) that we develop from infancy. We develop belief systems in four ways:

1) From the things we see.

2) From the things we hear.

3) From the individual events that we experience in our lives.

4) From our parents, friends, society, culture, teachers and the media.

The belief system you have about money is the most important factor in what will determine your use of it. That is why it is essential to discover what you believe deep down, where it has come from and to change it to a belief that will help you become and stay financially well. A question to ask yourself is - am I influencing my children in a positive or negative way with regards to money in what I constantly say to them?"

How to teach your child this important lesson

Ask your child to complete these three statements. I think money is ...... My parents say money is .... My friends say money is ....

Next, have him think about what he thinks about rich and poor people in general. Get him to answer the following two questions - Rich people are....... Poor people are ...... Explore where you or your child might have developed those beliefs about rich and poor people using the four ways we develop our beliefs as discussed above. If you discover that you or your child believes that rich = greedy, selfish, mean, evil, or bad, discuss with him why believing this about rich people may stop him, even subconsciously, from becoming rich (or financially well). Your thoughts, beliefs and attitudes will influence your wealth potential.

Could his (or your) opinion come from a good experience with money or a bad experience with money? The truth is that some poor people are greedy, selfish, and mean just as some rich people are. Henry Ford (the developer of the Ford motor vehicle) was a very rich man. He was also a very generous man and in fact the Ford Foundation still gives away hundreds of millions of dollars per year to various charities and organisations.

- **The spoken word is very powerful**
- **Be careful what you say about money and what you say about people who have or do not have much money**

Our financial life or any other area of our life can be transformed by renewing our mind with new positive information. Speaking out loud what you want to achieve is a way of helping change old thinking or beliefs you hold in your mind. Speaking out can help reinforce new ideas and concepts and increase the probability that your child will learn and incorporate these new ideas and concepts into his daily life.

Which of the following statements "I'll never get out of debt" or "I am working towards paying off my debt" will result in you being and staying financial well? It will be "I am working towards paying off my debt", because if you continuously say "I'll never get out of debt" then that is what will happen, because that is what you are continuously reinforcing.

Much of our thinking as adults was formed from what was spoken to us as children. Because we have all heard and possibly said things about money such as "I'll never get out of debt", we need to find a way to develop new thoughts about money which will help us become and stay financially well. Become aware of what you are saying about money and listen to what others are saying.

How to teach your child this important lesson

Both you and your child stand up, and say the following statements out loud. Have some fun. Listen to yourself as you say them, and think about what you are saying. The spoken word is very powerful.

You could make up other statements for other areas of you and your child's life. Try making up one for something they are having difficulty with. If you want a challenge, it could be something like "I am working towards keeping my room tidy every single day."

THE SILBO PRINCIPLES TO STAY FINANCIALLY WELL

- It's not chance but ***choice*** that determines my financial future
- My ***beliefs*** about money influence how I handle it
- It is ***my*** responsibility to stay financially well
- Being ***broke*** won't last forever, being ***poor*** is a state of mind
- Give away a portion of your income to ***help others***
- Find what you love to do and do it with ***passion*** and ***excellence***
- ***Save 10%*** of what you earn before you do anything
- ***Grow your money*** by putting it to work
- Making more money isn't always the answer. It's ***what I do*** with what I earn that matters
- Have written ***goals*** and ***review*** them regularly
- Interest is only ***good*** when I am ***getting*** it
- Save up for things so you can pay ***cash***
- ***Avoid*** hire purchases and personal loans
- Assets keep me ***financially well,*** liabilities keep me financially sick
- Do not borrow money for things that ***lose value***
- ***Tell*** your money where to go instead of wondering where it's gone
- Healthy money ***habits*** will put me on the path to ***financial freedom***
- ***Stick*** to a sharing, spending and savings plan
- When I ***borrow*** money I become a slave to my lender
- Being ***financially well*** will give me more choices
- ***Spend less*** than you earn by trimming expenses
- Don't put all the ***fruits*** of your labour into one basket
- Let your ***emotions*** subside then decide ***before*** spending your money
- Borrowing money for things that go down in value is ***dumb debt***
- Borrowing money for things that can go up in value is ***smart debt***

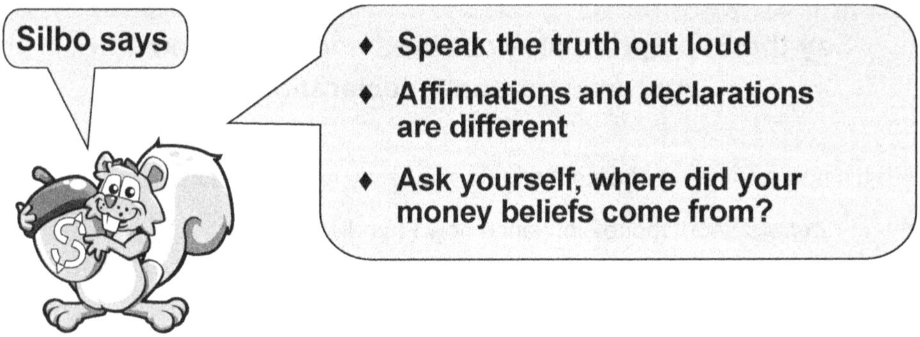

Speaking out a declaration or affirmation is a powerful way to change unhelpful beliefs. If you find you are speaking negatively about any situation, write down a new helpful belief and then speak it out daily. This is very powerful because as you read it, speak it and then hear what you have just said your subconscious will start to believe it is true.

The difference between declarations and affirmations is slight, but in my mind powerful. The definition of an **affirmation** is 'a positive statement claiming that a goal you wish to achieve is *already happening*'. For example, saying "I am totally out of debt" (when in fact you have a credit card bill of $5,000 that you can't pay completely right now). The trouble with this is when you affirm something that is not yet real, the little voice in your head usually responds with ("that is untrue, that is rubbish") and so sabotages your efforts to pay off your credit card.

The definition of a **declaration** is 'to state an *intention to undertake* a particular course of action.' If you decide you want to pay off your credit card and you increase your payments by $10 per week and put your credit card away the following declaration will be very powerful. "I am actively working towards paying off all my credit card debt by increasing my payments by $10 per week and putting my credit card away". Your little voice says "I can do this!" so this declaration becomes a true statement and reinforces your intention to get rid of your credit card debt.

Positive thinking or speaking about anything without any action to bring about change is just sending empty words into the air.

How to teach your child this important lesson

Go through the list on the following page and tick which ones are true for your child right now (affirmation) and reword the ones that are not true right now and make them a declaration. For example "I give away a portion of my income to help others". If you are not doing that right now you could change it to "I am going to give a portion of my income away to help others". You could make up other declarations for other areas of your lives. Try making up one for something you or your child are having difficulty with like doing homework, watching too much television, or keeping their rooms tidy.

Say the Silbo principles out loud and make them into your own personal declarations.

- It's not chance but ***choice*** that determines my financial future
- My ***beliefs*** about money influence how I handle it
- It is ***my*** responsibility to stay financially well
- Being ***broke*** won't last forever, being ***poor*** is a state of mind
- I give away a portion of my income to ***help others***
- Find what you love to do and do it with ***passion*** and ***persistence***
- ***I save 10%*** of everything I get
- **I grow my money** by putting it to work for me
- Making more money isn't always the answer. It's ***what I do*** with what I earn that matters
- I have written ***goals*** and ***review*** them regularly
- Interest is only ***good*** when I am ***getting*** it
- I always save up for things so I can pay ***cash***
- I ***avoid*** hire purchases and personal loans
- Assets keep me ***financially well,*** liabilities keep me financially sick
- ***I tell my money where to go*** instead of wondering where it's gone
- Healthy money ***habits*** will put me on the path to ***financial freedom***
- I ***stick*** to a sharing, spending and savings plan
- When I **borrow** money I become a **slave** to my lender
- Being **financially well** will give me more choices
- I **spend less** than I earn by trimming expenses
- I don't put all the ***fruits*** of my labour into one basket
- I let my ***emotions*** subside then decide ***before*** spending my money
- ***I do not*** borrow money for things that ***lose*** value
- Borrowing money for things that go down in value is ***dumb debt***
- Borrowing money for things that can go up in value is ***smart debt***

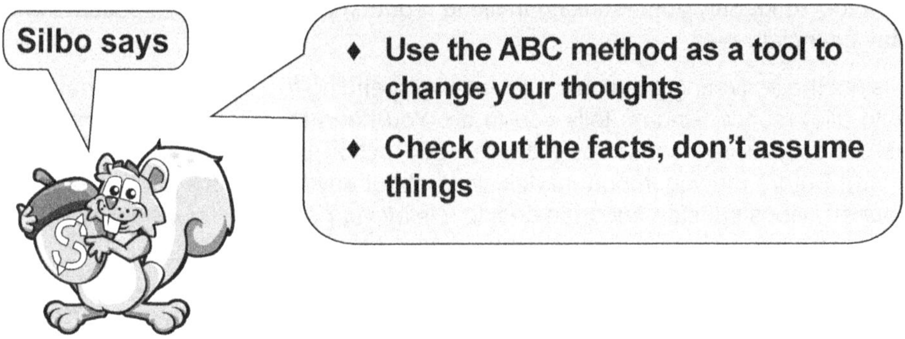

This lesson will help you and your child identify the reasoning behind some of your actions by understanding and using REBT (Rational Emotive Behaviour Therapy). Rational means showing evidence of clear and sensible thinking – not based on emotion or prejudice. Sometimes we assume the wrong thing which in turn leads to irrational (unreasonable thinking). REBT uses the A-B-C method to change irrational thinking.

Sometimes the only way to break a behaviour is to recognise that your actions come from beliefs in your conscious or subconscious thinking. In order to change those self defeating thoughts and actions about your finances, you need to understand how to turn those thoughts and beliefs around. REBT can help you do this. In other words to change the fruit (lack of money) you need to change the root (unhealthy thoughts about being financially well or sick). Although you cannot change the past, you can change how you let the past influence the way you are today and the way you want to be tomorrow. In this sense, REBT is an optimistic approach to living and to solving problems. Learning about the A-B-C method will set you and your child up in the future for being in control of their emotions instead of blaming others for what they "did" to them. For those who tend to act impulsively a helpful quote from Joyce Meyer is "Let emotions subside, then decide".

How to teach your child this important lesson

Read to your child (or have your child read through) the following information on the next page and talk him through the A-B-C process. Then get him to complete "You have a go". When we assume things – we can make big mistakes – check out the facts.

An interesting book to read is *"Choose to be Happy"* by Wayne Froggatt which explains Rational Emotive Behaviour Therapy. This book can be helpful for you to change other unhelpful beliefs you have which are not about money.

American psychologist Dr. Albert Ellis, the originator of Rational Emotive Behaviour Therapy, was one of the first to show how beliefs determine the way human beings feel and behave the way they do. He developed the A-B-C method of how to change self-destructive thinking.

The A-B-C method is a tool to change our thoughts. It helps us re programme our brains (or mental computers) so we can make more healthy choices. It can be a tool to identify your "stinking thinking" about money so you can become and stay financially well.

It is not the activating event that causes overspending for example, it is what your auto pilot (subconscious) tells you to do. You need to uncover those unhelpful beliefs so you can consciously choose and action better choices (renew your mind). Before making important decisions about anything, it is a good idea to let your emotions subside and then decide. *Delay your decision for 48 hours.*

How the A-B-C's work …

A = Activating Event   B = Belief   C = Consequence

"A" What started things off – something happens to you or someone does something.

"B" Possible beliefs about "A" - because of an underlying belief you have you will THINK a certain way.

"C" When you think in a certain way about something – that will determine how you react to that event.

When you have learned the ABC then you add D *(disagree)* & E *(exchange).*

When you have identified the belief that is a self defeating belief then *Disagree* with that belief then *Exchange* it for a new more life enhancing belief.

Look at the following example to see how the same event (car brakes need fixing) could have two different outcomes, because of a belief you might hold.

Example One

A **Activating event**	**B** **Belief**	**C** **Consequent feeling and action because of belief**
Car brakes need fixing	I need to buy a new car to save on future repairs.	Feeling – excited, enthusiastic, depressed.
	I need an expensive looking car to impress my friends.	Behaviour – look at cars without taking into account other expenses to run the car.
	This has worked out better than I hoped. It gives me an excuse to buy a new car.	Behaviour – irrational. Buy first car you look at.
	Buy now – pay later – don't worry about tomorrow and how much it will really cost.	Action - buy car on terms with a high interest rate at more than you can really afford.

Example Two

A **Activating event**	B **Belief**	C **Consequent feeling and action because of belief**
Car brakes need fixing.	Need to check out what is the best thing to do.	Feelings: Cautious,frustrated. Action: Check out the facts
	When I borrow money I become a slave to my lender.	Behaviour: Get quotes to get car fixed. Investigate price of new cars and how much the existing car will sell for.
	Interest is only interesting when I am receiving it.	Research interest rates and compare overall costs.
	Debt is bad.	Avoid getting a car on hire purchase unless absolutely necessary – eg I must have a car to do my job.

YOUR TURN NOW. Come up with your own ABC. Examples: Mum or Dad told you off for something you didn't do. You do well in a test at School. One of your friends calls you names. You miss a goal. You want to buy a new cell phone.

Sometimes because of our beliefs we ASSUME the wrong thing.

Fill in the blanks below.

A **Activating event**	B **Belief**	C **Consequent feeling and action because of belief**

Making assumptions can trip you up.
Check out the facts!

Silbo says

- **Think about your thinking**
- **You are responsible for your own decisions**
- **You can be taught to think more clearly**

Sometimes we make decisions based on what others think or before really checking out the facts. This page is designed to help you "think about what you are thinking". Dr. Edward de Bono believes that we can be taught to think more clearly to make better decisions. The following has been adapted from his website http://www.edwdebono.com and used with permission.

Sometimes our actions are because we are on auto pilot. As explained previously our beliefs are learned from our parents, friends, society, culture, teachers and the media and are formed from the things we see, the things we hear and from the individual events that we experience in our lives. We need a way to try and look outside the problem as if we were helping someone else make a good decision – based on facts, not purely on emotion.

How to teach your child this important lesson

Read the following where it explains about the six "Thinking Hats" and what their different colours mean.

White Hat Asks for facts & information. 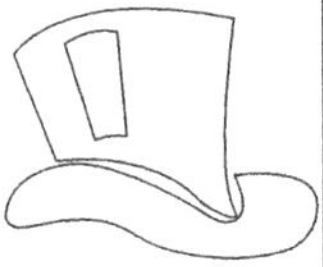	What information do we have? What information do we need? What do you know about the situation? What do you need to find out? Are these true facts or opinion? Where do we get the information?
Yellow Hat Looks at benefits & positive points 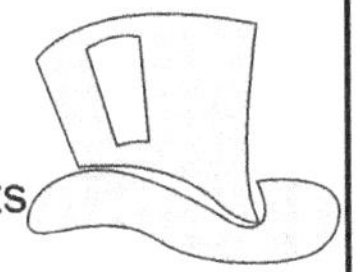	Yellow works out the 'how' and 'why' something will work and the benefits that will occur as a result of some proposed action.
Black Hat Caution & judgement. 	Probably the most valuable of the hats as it is used to point out why a suggestion does not fit the facts. It sets off warning bells and often prevents mistakes being made. What are the thinking errors? What may happen in the future? Does this fit past experience? Have I made these type of mistakes before?

Green Hat Creativity & new ideas.	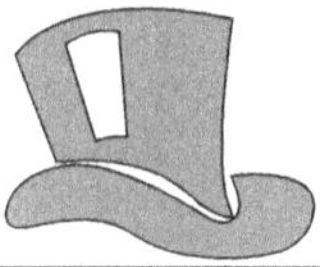	Green offers new ideas, concepts, and perceptions. The deliberate creation of new ideas. Humour and lateral thinking.
Red Hat Feelings & emotions.	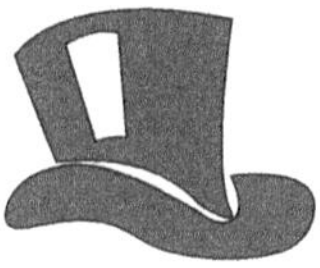	What is my gut reaction? What do I really feel about this? Emotion as logic. Using emotions as bargaining positions.
Blue Hat The thinking process.	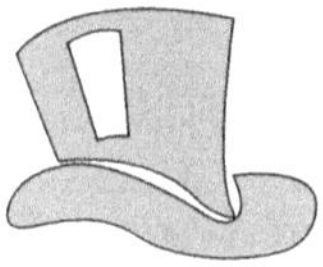	Thinking about thinking (why do I think that way?) Defining the problem. Is my thinking rational or irrational? Asking the right questions. The organisation of thinking – what should I think about first? Control of each hat – think with one hat at a time.

Now pretend to put on each coloured hat as you think about fixing the brakes on your car. Write down your thoughts as you answer each question. Examples of questions you could ask yourself could be "How much will the brakes cost? How much will be labour cost? Will I have to borrow money? Can anyone help me do it cheaper?"

White Hat Asks for facts & information.	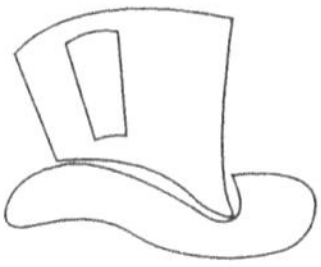	What information do we have? What information do we need? What do you know about the situation? What do you need to find out? Are these true facts or opinion? Where do we get the information?

Fact: the mechanic says the brakes need replacing to get a warrant of fitness.

Yellow Hat Looks at benefits & positive points	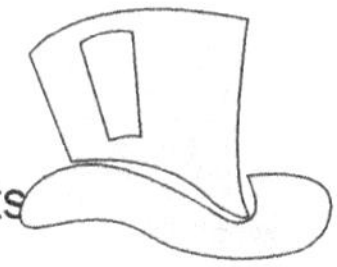	Yellow works out the 'how' and 'why' something will work and the benefits that will occur as a result of some proposed action.

Benefit: new brakes will make my car safer.

Black Hat Caution & judgement. 	Probably the most valuable of the hats as it is used to point out why a suggestion does not fit the facts. It sets off warning bells and often prevents mistakes being made. What are the thinking errors? What might happen in the future? Does this fit past experience? Have I made these type of mistakes before?

Caution: should I get a second opinion?

Green Hat Creativity & new ideas. 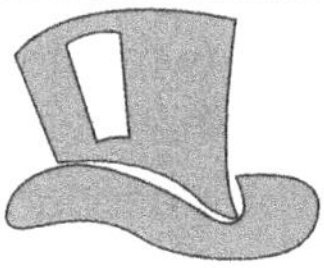	Green offers new ideas, concepts, and perceptions. The deliberate creation of new ideas. Humour and lateral thinking.

New idea: I could go to a mechanic's class and learn to fix it myself.

Red Hat Feelings & emotions. 	What is my gut reaction? What do I really feel about this? Emotion as logic. Using emotions as bargaining positions.

Emotion: I feel annoyed as I didn't plan for this.

Blue Hat The thinking process. 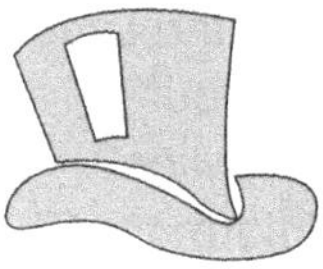	Thinking about my thinking (why do I think that way?) Defining the problem. Is my thinking rational or irrational? Am I asking the right questions? The organisation of thinking - what should I think about first? Control of each hat – think through problems with one hat at a time.

Thinking: Have I put each hat on and looked at the situation from all angles?

When you get into the habit of using the De Bono method for problem solving you will find your decision making is much more methodical and rational.

> **"The mind has exactly the same power as the hands: not merely to grasp the world, but to change it".**
> **Colin Wilson**

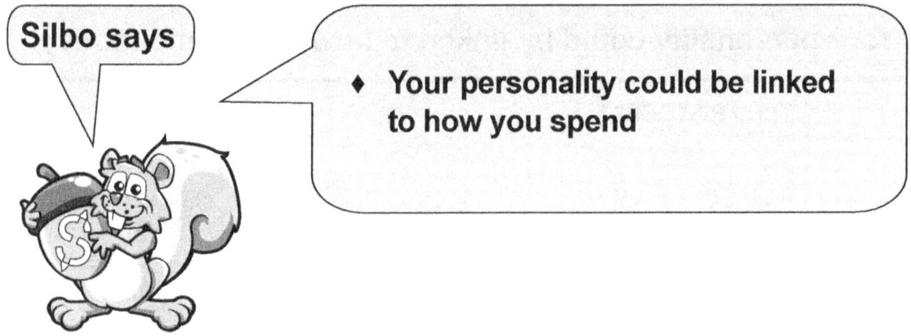

Just as research has shown that we are born with a dominant personality, studies have also shown that you could be born with a dominant money personality.

Knowing how your money personality shows up in your life may give you an understanding of why and how you and others handle money.

To explain six of the different money personalities I have used animals as a comparison.

Two other money personalities which I haven't mentioned are the "victim" type and the "rescuer" type. These two types of money personalities are at the opposite ends of the scale. Surprisingly enough they are often found together in relationships which work for a while until the person playing "victim" or the person playing "rescuer" decides they don't want to play this game anymore. The victim tends to blame others, live in the past, is financially irresponsible, wants to be rescued, is addictive, and feels powerless. For the victim's mentality to change he or she must learn to understand and heal past wounds from financial mistakes.

Whereas the "rescuer" loves to rescue, go guarantor, bails others out as they somehow feel responsible for their partner, relations or friends lack of financial intelligence. The rescuer needs to come to a place where they recognise they are really hindering the victim from realising they are responsible for their own good and bad financial decisions.

So which money personality do you most closely identify with? You could be a mixture of more than one and that is okay. Be careful about saying "I was born like that so there isn't anything I can do about it. You have a choice to be financially well or financially sick.

How to teach your child this important lesson

Have a look at the different money personalities with your child and get him to see if he recognises any of the traits in himself or in any member of the family (including you).

This can be a fun exercise to do with the whole family, friends and work colleagues to guess what money personality you think they could be.

Discuss one positive and one negative aspect of each personality.

Your personality could by linked to how you spend money

THE ARISTOCRAT

Cathy the Cat

Cathy thinks money isn't important and can't be bothered worrying about it. She has far too many other important things to do.

THE SAVER

Silbo the Squirrel

Silbo is a real squirrel and puts money away in case he needs to buy something. He loves to save and pay cash for things.

THE HOARDER

Harry the Hamster

Harry doesn't like spending money on anything. He lives very cheaply and refuses to share his wealth with anyone.

THE SPENDER

Mike the Monkey

Mike spends every cent he earns as soon as he gets it. He never saves and often spends more money than he makes.

THE AVOIDER

Dizzy the Duck

Dizzy Duck dives for cover the minute the bills arrive. She is always late making payments and often ends up in court for bad debts.

THE SAFETY PLAYER

Timid Thomas

Thomas is so afraid of making a mistake that he avoids making any financial decisions - even small ones.

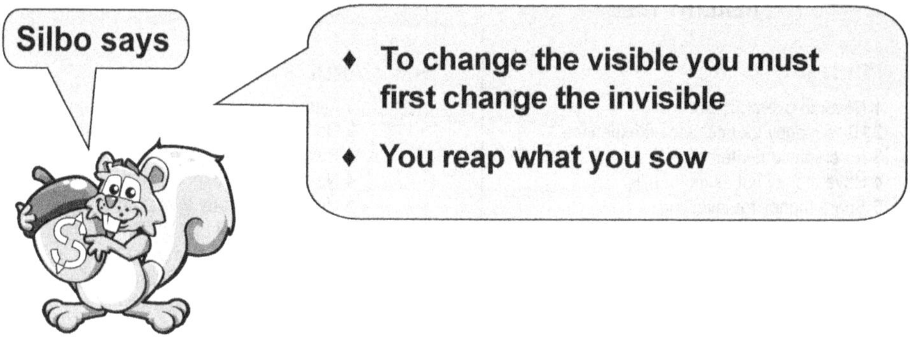

To change the visible – your current situation (good or bad), you must first uncover the habits and thoughts you have that lead you to being where you are. Once you have identified those habits and unhealthy thoughts you can go about replacing them with habits that will result in you being financially well.

You need to know what good habits will produce good fruit (an abundance of money) and what unhelpful habits will produce poor fruit (lack of money).

How to teach your child this important lesson

Have your child look at the "Silbo Money Tree " then discuss how those "healthy" and "sick" money fruits have resulted from those "healthy" and sick "roots".

Sometimes something can belong in both categories. An example is paying interest. If you are paying interest on a house which generally increases in value then paying interest can be a smart money move. However, paying interest for something like a stereo which decreases in value is a dumb money move.

Poor financial habits result in you being financially sick.

Healthy financial habits result in you being financially well.

HEALTHY TREE

FRUITS

1 Never in overdraft
2 Have money for unexpected expenses
3 No credit card interest
4 Have money put aside for bills
5 Spare money for investing

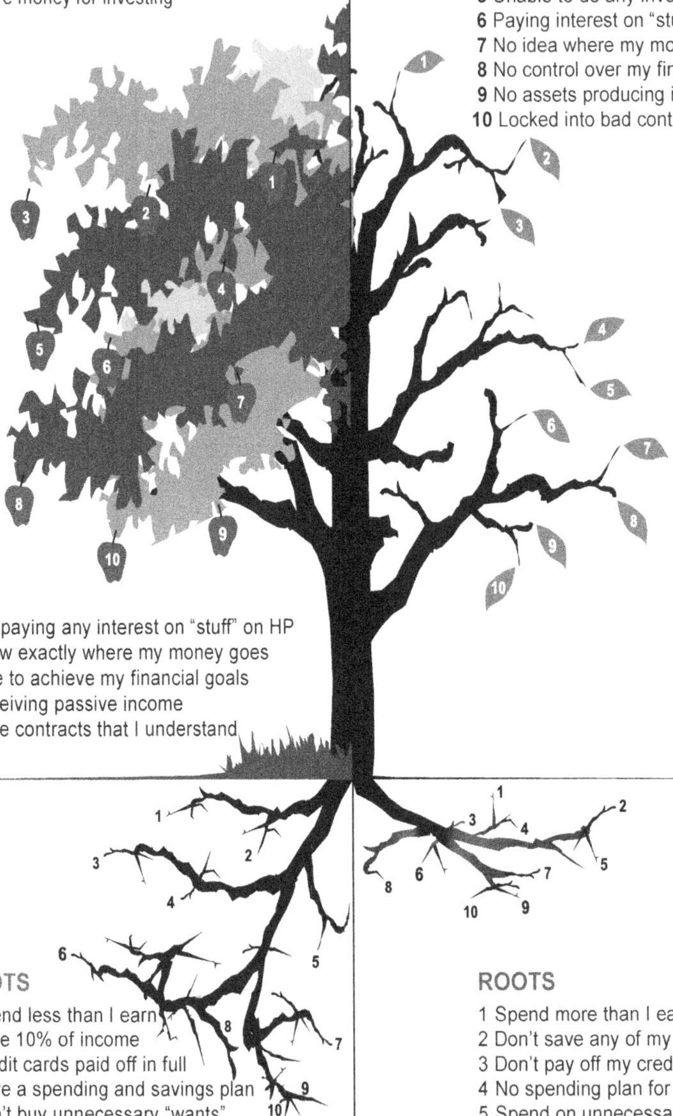

6 Not paying any interest on "stuff" on HP
7 Know exactly where my money goes
8 Able to achieve my financial goals
9 Receiving passive income
10 Have contracts that I understand

ROOTS

1 Spend less than I earn
2 Save 10% of income
3 Credit cards paid off in full
4 Have a spending and savings plan
5 Don't buy unnecessary "wants"
6 Don't put things on hire purchase
7 Always track where my money goes
8 Have SMART money goals
9 Own assets that produce passive income
10 Always read contracts before signing

SICK TREE

FRUITS

1 Always owing money
2 No money for unexpected expenses
3 Paying credit card interest
4 No money for bills
5 Unable to do any investing
6 Paying interest on "stuff' on HP
7 No idea where my money goes
8 No control over my financial future
9 No assets producing income
10 Locked into bad contracts

ROOTS

1 Spend more than I earn
2 Don't save any of my income
3 Don't pay off my credit cards
4 No spending plan for expenses
5 Spend on unnecessary "wants"
6 Have things on hire purchase
7 Don't track where my money goes
8 No financial goals
9 Own no income producing assets
10 Never read contracts before signing

To change the Fruits (visible) you have to change the Roots (invisible)

- **Myths (false beliefs) you believe about money can stop you being financially well**

There are many disempowering myths about money that could determine how money enters and leaves your life. These myths are formed from the culture you live in, your parents, friends and the media. In short, your financial reality is based on your identification with beliefs you hold about money. Every single belief you have around every part of the world you experience has this effect – it shapes your perception, which shapes your reaction to it and consequent actions.

The first step to uncovering what you may believe about money is to consciously think about your thinking to do with money. When you hear yourself talking about money – think consciously about what you are saying. You may have irrational thinking towards money.

A common false belief people have about money is "money is the root of all evil". If you believe that deep down, think for a moment how that could influence how you handle money. Most probably you will spend money as fast as you get it – because you don't want to handle that evil stuff. This myth has developed from many people misquoting a bible verse which says "The love of money is the root of all evil".

People who love money above everything else may do evil things to get money. Money can be anything you declare it to be – a tool to achieve great things, power in your pocket, a dirty piece of paper, a ticket to freedom, a ticket to unhappiness. Money can also be plentiful, abundant, it can be about freedom, choice, empowerment, value and goodness. Money can be a wonderful tool to help countries that have been ravaged by war, flood or famine. There are a lot of people who are willing to do bad things for money – the question here is, what do you believe and how does that belief affect your life day to day?

Money is just a thing, it is not 'living'. Your experience of it is an incredible powerful thing – it can be motivating, empowering, disempowering or demoralizing.

How to teach your child this important lesson

We need tools to help uncover what is underneath things to find the cause of what is happening on the surface. Like gardening, you use a spade to move the soil so you can see what is happening underneath. It can be likened to a tree which doesn't bear any fruit. Sometimes it is because the roots are root bound. The roots go round and round in circles, and the plant just doesn't thrive. It is the same if our roots (beliefs/myths) about money are all bound up, we too will go round and round in circles wondering why we are not making any progress financially.

The belief questionnaire about money is a tool to help you uncover those beliefs/ myths/roots that you probably didn't know you had. You can change them for beliefs that will help you become and stay financially well.

Go through the belief questionnaire with your child and rate yourselves what you believe from 1 – 10 with regard to each of the following statements.

1=100% strongly disbelieve, up to 10 = 100% strongly believe

Belief Questionnaire

BELIEF	SCORE
I believe money is the root of all evil	
I believe money is a pain	
I believe that other people need my money more than I do	
I believe I am not good enough to be wealthy	
I believe being financially well is more good luck than good management	
I believe the rich are getting richer and the poor are getting poorer	
I believe that there is no point in being the richest person in the cemetery	
I believe I should leave a reasonable inheritance for my children	
I believe my children shouldn't get any financially help from me	
I believe that money isn't important	
I believe that there is not much point earning more money because I will just have to pay more taxes	
I believe that I shouldn't make more money than my parents	
I believe if I were rich my friends would not like me	
I believe it is much harder for a women to become financially independent	
I believe you can't get rich if you are honest	
I believe God will make me, rich, poor or middle class	

BELIEF	SCORE
I believe you need a scam to get rich	
I believe if I wasn't born into a financially well family I will always be financially sick	
I believe I should always give but never receive	
I believe giving a portion of my income to charitable causes is a mistake	
I believe money is something to be enjoyed	
I believe money causes lots of problems for everyone	
I believe money can't buy you happiness	
I believe rich people are greedy, selfish and stuck up	
I believe money is something I don't have	
I believe rich people are unhappy	
I believe having a lot of money is too big a responsibility	
I believe I need to have an expensive car or house so people will think I am successful	
I believe money doesn't grow on trees. Money is scarce	

Now read through some of the popular myths about money – adapted from a the following website http://www.chrisj.winisp.net/freedom/myths.htm and read the explanations as to why they are indeed myths. After you have finished reading, re-do the belief questionnaire and think about where you can change some of your old unhelpful beliefs for more helpful beliefs. These new beliefs will empower you to stay financially well.

Another website to look up about myths is http://ihatedebt.com/

"MONEY IS THE ROOT OF ALL EVIL"

This is an unhelpful declaration about money. It is saying money is something to be feared. This is not rational (showing evidence of clear thinking).

Money can be anything we declare it to be. A tool in your hands, power in your pocket, a ticket to freedom, a dirty piece of paper or evil. Take your pick - it is what you make of it.

Yes, there are a lot of people out there who are willing to do bad things for money. The question we're concerned with here is what does having this perspective do to you? Choosing a good relationship with your money is important, because your relationship to it determines how you experience it.

On the other hand there are many people who are willing to do good things for money and many people who are wealthy who choose to be very generous in supporting organisations which help solve problems like homelessness and hunger.

So, is money dirty? From a certain perspective, sure. (You can get dirty hands if you pick up money that is dirty). It is not evil – because evil is in the hearts of men, not in their wallets. If you limit your view to that perspective, that's what you'll see and that's the reality you'll create for yourself. *Money can also be plentiful, abundant, it can be about freedom, choice, empowerment, value and goodness.* If you choose these relationships to it, your perception of money will change and if that change empowers you or makes you happy, that can only be a good thing.

"MONEY DOESN'T GROW ON TREES/MONEY IS SCARCE"

Obviously, money doesn't grow on trees... but what is meant here is that getting hold of it isn't as simple as walking out the front door and filling a basket with the stuff.

We all heard this from our parents when we wanted something and they decided that it was an inappropriate use of their money. We might even hear it coming out of our own mouths when we feel that we don't have enough money to get something we want. This is the voice of defeat, telling you that something is impossible.... but what does this belief do to you? If you believe it, you will validate it. You will be 'right', and your ego likes to be right. Your ego gets a lot of validation out of being 'right', and your ego will make it tough to question this belief - and if you agree with this belief, chances are that it will become true.

The reality is that money itself is a made-up thing, used to measure the value of whatever it is that you create and deliver to others, and therefore money is potentially infinite.

"MONEY IS SOMETHING I DON'T HAVE"

If this is your identity, if it is how you view yourself, it's tough to go against - it feels a lot like proving yourself wrong, which can be a bit painful. Your subconscious doesn't like that kind of pain, and will push you relentlessly in order to validate it. From your subconscious view, if this myth is part of your reality, it is necessary to be rid of your money in order to demonstrate self-love. In truth, however, *you are not your money and your money cannot define you.*

"MONEY IS NOT IMPORTANT"

If you choose to neglect your 'unimportant' money, you'll certainly be free of it.

There is a significant difference between focusing on money and neglecting the rest of your life and the things you value. Unfortunately, this myth seems to equate focusing on money with neglecting other valuable things, when this is never true. If your interpretation of this myth leads you to neglect your financial health, sooner or later your poor financial health will become a problem. This is

Money is like a friend - if you don't treat it right, it'll go away.

a question of balance. Certainly there are other things that are important, but your financial health is important too! Getting rid of your money won't help you value your friends more, it will just leave you without money and that can put other strains on your relationships.

If you focus "only" on money, you won't do well - your friends will rightly think you're out of whack. If you ignore your money, you won't do well either - you'll have none. Somewhere in the middle is a balanced, functional place.

Life isn't all about "having things". It can be helpful to have enough money to do the things that feed your spirit. For example if you love to walk on the beach or help someone else because that's what makes you feel really good, less depressed etc., then it is helpful to have some spare money for petrol to take you to the beach – so you can care about yourself.

"MONEY CAN'T BUY HAPPINESS/MONEY WON'T MAKE YOU HAPPY"

Money can't buy happiness, but it sure can't hurt. Lack of money, on the other hand, can make things a bit harder. Money means different things to all of us, power, safety, freedom, independence, stature, control and these ideas form the roots of our relationship with money.

In a very literal way, this statement is entirely true, you can't buy happiness with money. At the same time, the statement is confusing and a lot of people come away from it with different conclusions, that money is unimportant, or that money is the problem and getting rid of it is the solution.

"I CAN'T AFFORD IT"

If you believe that you can't afford it, it will become true because you'll never try to get it. Or even think that it may be possible. It's really that simple, and this myth puts you on the back foot. However, if what you want to do or buy isn't in your sharing, spending and savings plan then saying "I choose to stick to my sharing, spending and savings plan" will be an empowering statement as it is putting you in control.

"IF I WERE RICH, MY FRIENDS WOULD RESENT ME"

Friends who resent their friends' success aren't friends. Straight up - friends who block friends' attempts to succeed financially have some unhelpful issues around money themselves.

If you conform to their desires, you're letting them down, and that's not the work of a friend. If they become uncomfortable with your desire to succeed, you know for a fact that you'd be doing them a favour by succeeding - you'd help them get past that blocked part of themselves.

If you hold yourself back from success in order to 'be accepted by your friends', you're doing nobody any favours. You're letting them down, and worse, you're failing yourself by not trying to succeed.

"I'LL SAVE MONEY WHEN I HAVE ENOUGH"

Any amount of money you save, no matter how small, is enough to save. The habit of saving money is more important than the amount. My sister, who at the time was a solo parent made a decision to put away every 50 cents that came into her hands into a piggy bank for her son. She did this without fail into a paper mache pig she and her son had made. The amount grew and was such a great boost to her son's bank account and a wonderful example for her son to follow. Habits are incredibly powerful things. Her son started saving when he first got a job and was able to buy a house and then fully pay it off by the time he was 32 years old. He is now married with two small children and his wife is able to stay at home with their children by choice because he owned his home without any debt.

"YOU NEED A BREAK TO BECOME WEALTHY"

Wealth is not an accident, it's a function of your actions in your financial world - and your actions are directly shaped by your thoughts, feelings, and beliefs around money, value and business. We've all heard stories about how lottery winners manage to lose all of their winnings, and how multimillionaires who lose everything tend to rebuild their wealth within years. Wealth is not an accident, nor is it a function of luck - it is a function of your actions in life, and your motives. Some people use "you need a break" as a way to avoid being responsible for how their lives turned out.

"YOU NEED A SCAM TO GET RICH"

If you honestly believe that the only way to make money is in unethical behaviour, you will not look for ethical ways to make money, it's as simple as that. Your mind is closed. Opportunities for business exist, they are out there everywhere but in your subconscious mind you "believe that none of them are right for you".

This belief is a self-fulfilling prophecy, if you buy into it. If you think there must be a scam involved, you won't look at your legitimate opportunities because you believe "you need a scam to get rich".

"MONEY IS A BURDEN/MONEY IS A BIG RESPONSIBILITY"

If you think of money as a burden, you will find a way not to have that burden - our minds are like that. You will pass on business opportunities, stick with your current job because it's safe and avoid modelling the behaviour of successful people. You will resist learning how to make money easily. Instead, you'll limit your experience with money to that of working for other people, working for the bank, working for the tax collector, and in truth you will only relate to money in the sense that it is a burden. If you think of money as a burden, it will become a burden to you, even if you manage to become wealthy. You'll end up working hard to keep it, rather than finding ways for it to maintain itself and grow by itself, because if you 'know' that it's a burden, you won't look for ways for your money to be easy.

If you invest and create passive income streams, your money can create ease and abundance in your life. If you believe that it can be a tool to accomplish what you want, you will find ways for it to do that - if you do not, you won't. Again, this myth is a powerful and self-fulfilling thing.

"IT'S BETTER TO GIVE THAN TO RECEIVE"

Giving is a good thing, something I enjoy quite a bit - but there's nothing wrong with receiving either because for every gift given, there must be a recipient. Being a bad receiver doesn't make you a bad person, or for that matter, a bad giver - it just makes you uncomfortable about receiving.

If you're uncomfortable about receiving things, you'll find ways not to - whether it's gifts, income, anything. *You may avoid profitable situations that deliver value to others, simply in order to avoid receiving.* An important skill to have if you want to become financially well, is in being able to receive as gracefully as you give. I think a more accurate interpretation of the saying "It's better to give than to receive" is "You are doubly blessed by giving". When you give you get satisfaction as you bless someone and you are blessed because you have enough of something to be able to share in the first place.

"THE RICH ARE GETTING RICHER, WHILE THE POOR ARE GETTING POORER"

What's interesting in the context of this discussion is this question: "What does believing this myth do to you? What do you get out of this belief? How does this belief benefit/harm you?"

In a system where people are free to choose how they make their money, some of us will make mistakes. As long as people are free, any one in any financial situation can move from the bottom tier to the top tier. Are the rich getting richer? Who are the rich? Who are the poor? How does this apply to you and me? According to the treasury, most of us change chairs many times before the end of the dance - and all of this is probably only important to you in the sense that the way you choose to interpret this data can help or hinder you. Does the fact that the top earners are moving faster than the bottom earners encourage or discourage you from joining them?

"RICH PEOPLE ARE GREEDY"

Aside from the fact that this is a broad generalisation, it's also not really true. The simple truth is that it's terribly difficult to make money if you're not generous. Huh? Yes, generous. How does that work? In every transaction, there must be value for both participants of the transaction, or else it doesn't work. The easiest way for anyone to become wealthy is by creating a means to give the most value to the greatest number of people possible, at the least possible cost. If your product or service doesn't give your customer enough value for your price, they will go elsewhere and you will not make money. If you're not generous with the value you create, if you're not constantly looking for ways to deliver more value to more people for less money, you will find it much more difficult to become rich.

Resenting rich people is a trap, not only because it makes you unhappy over something not in your control, but also because it will prevent you from modelling their behaviour. You don't want to become like someone you dislike, right? Your ego would never tolerate that. If you became like someone you disliked wouldn't all your friends dislike you?

It's a trap, and it will give you reasons that will keep you from becoming successful with money.

The truth is that most wealthy people are admirably generous - not only do they create and deliver value to as many people as they can, as a group they give more, more often to charities and causes than any other group can. Another truth is that we're easily blinded to this by jealousy.

"RICH PEOPLE DON'T CARE ABOUT THE POOR"

Some people would say to demonstrate care is to open their wallet and give the poor money, because they have more than they do. There are problems that money just can't solve, and although it may be difficult to swallow, being poor is one of them if a person chooses to be that way say from having a drug habit.

I am not talking here about the poor from countries that have been ravaged by war or famine. I believe by giving to organisations such as Tear Fund or World Vision who give people a help up not a handout is a wonderful way of making a difference in a poor person's life. Many rich people give generously to organisations such as these. If a person lacks money, how can they give what they do not have?

At the bottom line, lack of money is a symptom, rather than a cause, of poverty. People who are financially strapped are that way for a reason, and giving them money will never touch that reason. All it will do is enable them to avoid solving the problem that's making them poor.

If your idea of caring is to treat the symptoms of a problem, this is probably a theme in your life that recurs. Do friends and family borrow from you? Come to you with problems that they have caused by misusing what money they do have, and expect you to fix it by giving them money? Are you uncomfortable with saying "no" when it is not treating the root of the problem?

Bringing it all together

Okay, so we've seen all of these myths and we can see that many of them create for us a reality that is limiting. Perhaps you don't want those limits for yourself any more. They may have been right for you once, but maybe now you're ready for a different set of beliefs. The good news is that you've just taken the first step. What you've begun to do is to think about the way you view your world, the way your past experiences and conclusions have shaped your present perspectives and beliefs, and to question whether you know more now than you did when you arrived at your particular belief. *This process of revisiting your beliefs is the first step toward putting the reins of your life into the hands of your present self, rather than leaving them in the hands of your past self.*

From here on, if you decide that you want to, you'll begin to notice how you relate to your beliefs - you'll begin to actively think about subjects that normally you wouldn't question. You'll make it a habit to try to understand and question your own beliefs and if you're like me you'll decide that many of your beliefs don't fit you any more. Think about what your childhood was like. Was it one where you lived in a constant state of terror, anxiety and turmoil? If it was, you may subconsciously create chaos in your own life by overspending or gambling so that you live your life how you subconsciously "believe" it should be. Sometimes, counselling can help uncover what is causing you to go round and round in circles.

If you think about it, this could be one of the most valuable things you ever do for yourself. Your beliefs come from conclusions you drew from your experiences in the past. Your conclusions have always been coloured by your beliefs, and so your belief system, your personal mythology, is "your own creation" - and it isn't right or wrong, it is just what worked for you at the time. You not only have the right to change it, you have the obligation to change it if it doesn't serve you.

The practical upshot of all of this is that your habits are a function of your beliefs. If your beliefs don't serve you, neither will your habits. If your habits don't serve you, you'll spend a lot of your energy working towards what you want, fighting against the force of your own habits. If your habits serve you, however, success will become automatic and effortless, whether you choose to focus on money, your relationships, or whatever you do.

"The mint makes it first, it's up to you to make it last."
Evan Esar

Silbo says

- **Advertisers will appeal to your emotions to get you to buy**

Often you buy things because they appeal to one of your emotions and feelings, such as the thing is going to make you feel better or look better. You will end up buying something not because you really need it but because your emotions tell you that you want it. In order to know if you are making a decision based on sensible buying or buying something based on an emotional feeling you have to be able to recognise the real reason you are being drawn to the object or thing.

Often after the purchase, and reality sets in, the happy feeling quickly disappears when you face the fact that because of your actions you now have say $30 per week less to spend on food. This can be a very unpleasant "wake up call" when you may have already been finding it difficult to buy the basic food necessities each week.

How to teach your child this important lesson

Go through the different emotions and feelings below and see how many adverts you can think of that use those emotions and feelings to try and get you to buy their product. Have a look at different magazines and try and recognise the emotion and feelings they are appealing to.

Next time you are watching television, play a game of trying to recognise the emotion or feeling they are trying to appeal to. Discuss it openly as a family.

Think of different advertisements you have seen that use these emotions and feelings to try and get you to buy their product or get you to do something.

Repetition	**Health and well-being**	**Feeling good**
Use of fear	**Lack of something**	**Security**
Popularity	**Power**	**Value**
Being new	**Freedom**	**Fun**
Humour	**Sexy**	**Convenience**
Jingles – music	**Comfort**	**Excitement**

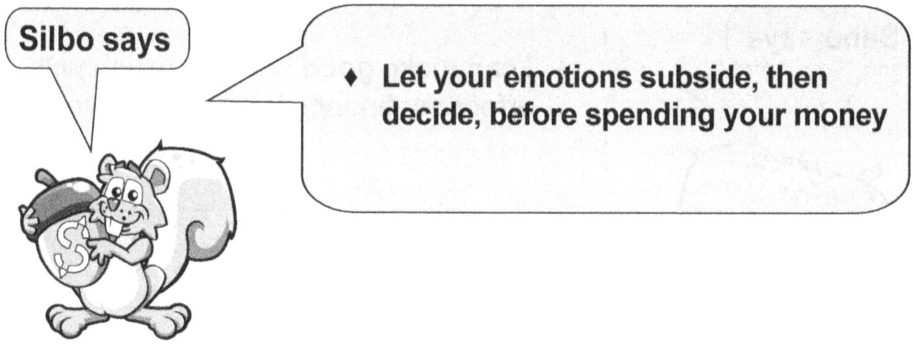

We all have individual characters and gifts that make us unique. By exploring how we think about ourselves and what makes us happy, we are able to put our lives in the right order to enable us to attain the things that are important to us.

Many people believe that they must **have** lots and be **do**ing lots of things in order for them to **be** happy. They will be trying to copy someone else or be like some one else because they think that is how you get happiness. The reality is that when we know who we are and can *be happy with <u>who</u> we are,* we can then move forward and start *to <u>do</u> the things we like* and to *<u>have</u> the things we want.*

How to teach your child this important lesson

Have a look at the words BE, DO, HAVE and talk with your child about how he feels about himself. Explore what makes your child unique and some of his strengths. How can he use these strengths to be able to do or have some of the things he wants? What does he think will make him happy? How long does he think that happiness will last? Is he trying to be like someone else? Does he think that person is happy?

Explain how many people try all their lives to be like someone else and often never find happiness. Sometimes people can accumulate great wealth or have lots of people around them or become powerful in the business world, but we hear how they were never happy because they were always trying to fill emptiness in their lives and never really knew who they were in themselves.

BE DO HAVE

BE, DO, HAVE adapted from the book
"One Minute Millionaire"
by Mark V Hansen and Robert G Allen

- **I can make good choices which will affect my financial future positively**

There are many choices in life to be made. Sometimes the hardest choice is making the decision, then once the choice is decided it is easier to progress down the chosen road.

If you are undecided and dithering about which way to go, the world will pass you by and opportunities will be lost. With your financial future at stake, it is important that you take the time to reflect on what you want for your life and where you want to go. If you decide you want to go down the path of financial wellness then first comes the decision, then comes some action.

How to teach your child this important lesson

Look at the next page and discuss how your child's choices in life can have an impact on his future. Look at the two sides (left and right columns) and talk about where each side (choice) might lead him. The left side will lead to being financially sick and the right side to being financially well.

You can talk about your own financial choices you have made and how they have influenced where you are today.

"We can try to avoid making choices by doing nothing, but even that is a decision." <u>Gary Collins</u>

Financially sick

Expensive Cars with
big repayments and
insurance costs

Stuff that decreases
in value when
you buy it

Huge homes and
big mortgages when
not financially well

I

C__________

TODAY

WHAT

I WANT

FOR

TOMORROW

Financially well

Home with no Debt

Stock Market

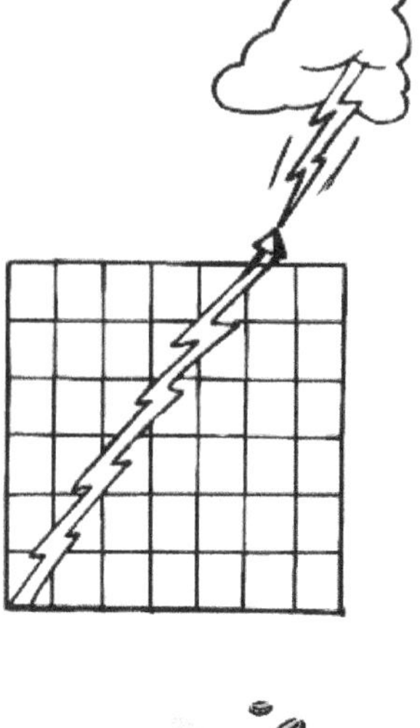

Property that gives
me Passive Income

Silbo says

- **Don't just wait for things to happen**
- **Make a choice**

Reaching towards being and staying financially well is a choice and the responsibility for making it happen belongs with each individual once they make that choice.

Succeeding at anything is virtually impossible unless you set it as a goal first and choose it.

How to teach your child this important lesson

Have your child draw up a simple statement like the one below and if he chooses have him sign his name to it and date it. You could put it on the wall and frame it as reminder of the decision made.

What I choose today will take me to where I want to be tomorrow

I choose for me and my family to be and stay financially well

__________________________ ____________________

Your Signature **Date**

Step 3

> **"We make a living by what we get, we make a life by what we give."**
> **<u>Sir Winston Churchill</u>**

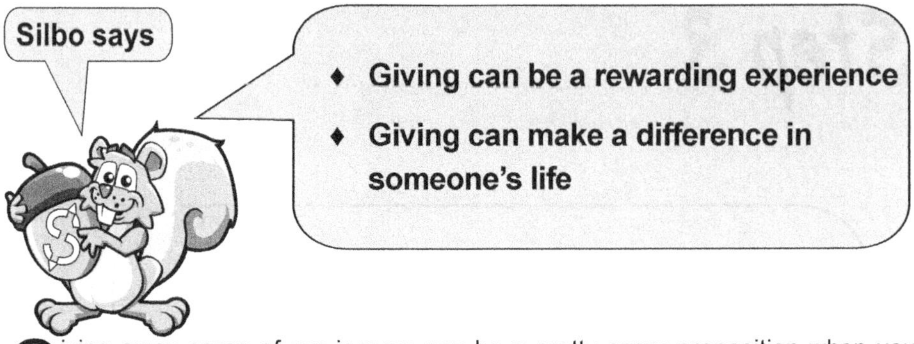

Giving away some of our income can be a pretty scary proposition when you know you have worked hard to get it in the first place. Sharing with others is an important part of life. The act of giving away the first 10% of your income is a well known and recognised principle (commonly known as tithing) that has been around for thousands of years. It is still practiced today by many groups. Whether you give away or share 10%, or 5% or 20% of your income isn't the main issue. It is that you develop an attitude of thinking of others. It also isn't all about money, as you may give your time helping an elderly person with some gardening or donating food to a food bank. When you give money it shows that you are in control of your money instead of it controlling you.

Much of today's society focuses on "getting" as much money or "stuff" as we can. However, a large section of our world's population depends on the giving of others so they don't starve. Whether it is money, food, or manpower the principle of sharing and giving to others is an important part of the make up of the world we live in. Teaching your children to think of others by giving prepares them for adult life and can protect them from having a "freeloader" mentality of always expecting others to provide for them. When they are trained in the habit of regular giving and sharing, they are then more naturally inclined to think of others first and have a more charitable outlook on life.

How to teach your child this important lesson

With your child, have a look at organisations in the community that help and support others. Some examples may be Red Cross, Asthma Foundation, Salvation Army, Tear Fund, Ruel Foundation or your local church. Discuss how you and your child can support one of these or another organisation. Have a look at how your child's contribution could change lives by discussing how all the little amounts when added together, can become a significant amount and then can make a difference in someone's life. Make a list of all the different organisations in your community who are supported with donations of time and money so they can help people. Most local libraries and citizen advice bureaus have a list of community organisations.

There are many organisations that feed the poor overseas. One organisation *www.joycemeyerministries.com* on its website states that they can feed, educate and share the gospel for one person for $6 per month. That is in American dollars. That is 19 American cents per day! Discuss how because the New Zealand dollar is worth a lot more money in some other countries, that by donating a small amount of money it can make a real difference in the life of someone overseas.

Sharing with others is an important part of life. The act of giving away the first 10% of your income is a well known and recognised principle.

Look at some of these organisations and think about how they help others in society. You may think "How can my little amount make a difference?" Many little amounts added together make up a large amount and that can make the difference in someone's life.

Find out about these organisations and write down what they do with the money or resources that are given to them. Think of another organisation that helps others. Do they need finances, or do they need a helping hand?

The Salvation Army

The Red Cross

Medical supplies

First Aid staff

Emergency Help

Famine Aid

Humanitarian aid

Ruel Foundation

Tear Fund

TEAR Fund
Christian Action

The local church

Name another organisation that needs some help.

What do they need?
Can you help?

"It's not how much we give, but how much love we put into giving."
Mother Teresa

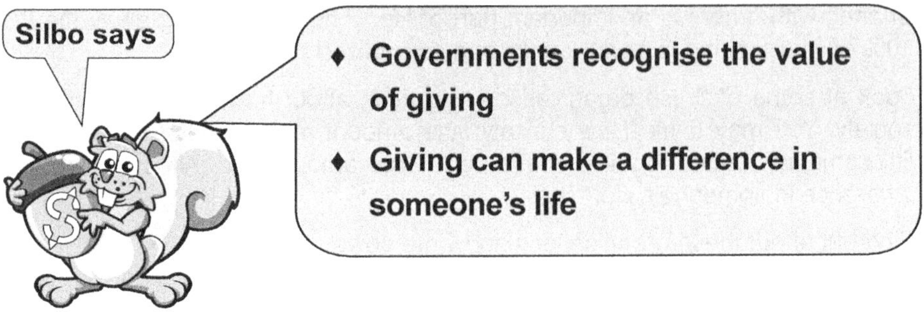

Philanthropists have a desire to improve the material, social, and spiritual welfare of humanity, especially through charitable activities. Many community organisations rely on individual's donations to supplement what that particular organisation may receive from Government organisations. Keep the receipts you have paid to a registered charitable trust so you can claim back some tax you have paid to the Government. This is where "giving and receiving" go hand in hand as the Government will give you back as a tax refund a percentage of every dollar you give to a registered charitable organisation.

The New Zealand Government recognises the value of people who give to charity (philanthropists) by allowing them to get a rebate of some of the tax they have paid on the money that they have donated to approved charities. Charitable giving, whether of time or money, makes an invaluable contribution to the wellbeing of any country. The New Zealand Government budget in 2007 removed the cap on the dollar amount of charitable donations that are eligible for tax relief. As of 2008, individuals can claim tax rebates up to the level of their taxable income, while companies and Maori authorities can claim deductions for donations up to the level of their annual net income.

The Australian Government, the British Government and the American Government also recognise the benefits of charitable donations. They each have a slightly different system for rewarding contributions made to recognised charitable organisations.

> In Australia donors can claim tax deductions for gifts made to eligible gift recipients. Entities entitled to receive tax deductible gifts are called deductible gift recipients (DGRs). A tax deduction for most gifts is claimed in the tax return for the income year in which the gift is made.
>
> In the United Kingdom, gifts to United Kingdom charities can be made through the payroll system. The amount can be deducted from your wages before tax is deducted which in effect reduces the amount of tax you have to pay.
>
> In America charitable donations can be tax deductible if made to qualified organisations and are made on the relevant tax form (depends on the amount of the donation as to which form is used).

How to teach your child this important lesson

Work through the example of a person who earns $600 net per week and who gives $60 per week to a registered charitable organisation to find out how much money they will get back from the Government. Explain how important it is to keep receipts for any money you donate because if you don't the Inland Revenue Department (tax department) will disallow your deduction and you just waste money that you could either save or give again to a worthy purpose. When you give to a registered charitable organisation they should give you a receipt either at the time or at the end of the financial year.

Example: Imagine that you earn $600 net per week and you give $60 per week to a registered charitable organisation.

1. You give $60 per week to a charitable organisation. Over the year that adds up to $3120.

2. At the end of the tax year that organisation gives you a receipt for all your donations.

3. You fill in a form IR526 from the Inland Revenue Department (IRD) and send it to them with the receipt for your donations of $3120 to claim back a third of that donation.

4. The IRD sends you a cheque or direct credits your bank account with $1040 which is a third of $3120.

Work out how much you will get back if you donate $1500 over the year.

$1500 divided by 33.3% (divided by 1/3) = $_______________

You are **throwing away** 33 cents in every dollar of the amount you donated if you do not claim your donation rebate.

Remember to keep all your donation receipts

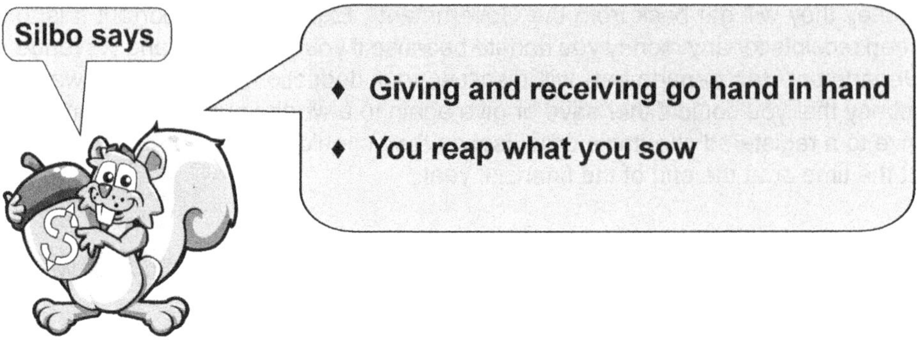

Just like the law of gravity – the law of giving works in the same way. It works even though we don't fully understand how it works.

People with a scarcity mindset think that if they give 10% of their income they will only have 90% left. They look at what they have given as if they have lost it for ever.

However, people who give from an attitude of gratitude and an abundance mindset think that if they give something away that it will come back to them multiplied. This is also another universal principle – you reap what you sow. The principle of reaping and sowing works not only with money but everything in life. If you sow friendship you receive friendship. If you cheat someone, someone will cheat you.

Like everything in life, it is important to live a life of balance. The act of giving should be part of your overall plan for your income which includes saving, sharing and spending. You can't make poor financial decisions today and expect to be rich tomorrow.

The universal law of giving to benefit others will ultimately enrich the life of the giver. The action of giving to others puts into place the mechanism for you to receive. It opens the pathway for your giving to be returned to you ten fold. Sometimes in the form you gave, other times in a way totally unexpected. Giving needs to come from the heart, not with the intention of giving so that you receive. Sometimes the biggest gift you can give to somebody is simply a smile!

How to teach your child this important lesson

Try and recount an experience where you have given to someone or something, then later have something really good happen to you. How did it feel? Have your child try and recall where he has helped a friend, then later have that friend or someone else help him. Ask him how they felt about that. Ask your child if he knows anyone who seems to be naturally generous. What characteristics about this person's giving give that impression?

Get your child to think about this statement. "One's acts of generosity might even be compared to planting a seed in the ground. It is not until after many days what was planted comes to maturity and yields a rich harvest".

Step 4

"Live neither in the past nor in the future, but let each days work absorb your entire energies, and justify your widest ambition."
Sir William Osler

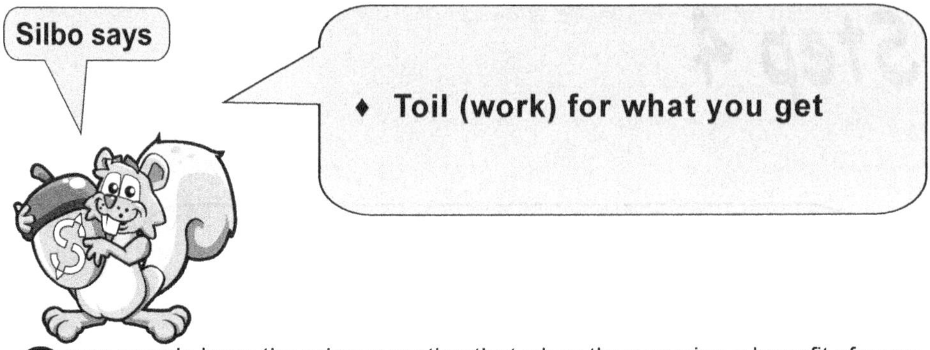

Some people have the misconception that when they receive a benefit of some description from the Government then that is how they "earn" their money. The word "earn" in the dictionary means "make money by working". Working means being engaged in paid or voluntary work. Sometimes it is necessary for people to receive a benefit because of illness or being temporarily unemployed, because they aren't able to work. However, many people get used to living on a benefit and lose sight of why it is good for them to get their money by working. Some countries have the policy "if you don't work you don't eat". Think about this *"Look at a day when you are supremely satisfied at the end. It is not a day when you lounge around doing nothing. It's a day when you have had everything to do, a real challenge, and you've done it."* (Quote from The little green book by John J P Elliot).

Some people think they are better off financially on a benefit because they only look at the "cash" that it costs them to go to work. They do not consider the benefits that they may gain by working, and where that work may lead them to in the future. Earning is learning. By working to earn your own money, you'll be learning skills you'll need to succeed in the world. These skills can include things like dealing with money, understanding what customers want and need, getting along with people, using tools and technology, using your time and materials wisely and many more. Money gives you choices. If you want to see a movie, get that great video game, or go out for burgers with your friends, you'll need cash to do it. Money you earn for yourself is yours to spend as you choose. Independence is a great feeling. It beats being bored. How many times have you been bored out of your skull, sitting around the house, convinced that there's absolutely nothing to do? Well, how about coming up with a plan to earn some money? That can be a great way to break through the boredom. By using your brain and your body to do jobs and make cash, you'll get energized, have a good time, and make the hours fly by. Resist the temptation from TV, radio, and magazine ads that may be telling you the opposite, which is spend spend spend. After the fun is gone, the money is, too!

How to teach your child this important lesson

Not all governments in all countries pay benefits to people when they are unemployed, or are sick. A good activity to do with your child, is to research into welfare systems in countries such as Thailand, so that they can see that if they live in New Zealand and need to get a benefit for some reason, that they are very fortunate.

Get your child to consider questions under the following headings.

What are some good things I could gain by working?

What skills could I gain from working?

What relationships could I gain from working?

How could my working benefit others?

Will working get me to financial freedom quicker?

It is better to have tried and found you didn't like it, than to have not tried and always wondered "what if".

Find what you love to do and do it with passion and persistence.

- **Find what you love to do and do it with passion**
- **Career planning has a valuable role to play in your life**

It is important that you allow your child to be who they are and not what you want them to be. Many adults are in careers that they hate but because there has been a family tradition in the past of being a lawyer, or a farmer etc they have felt obligated to follow this path and are miserable.

When you take into account what you or your child loves to do, that can be an excellent place to start when career planning. AC Nielsen research provides solid evidence of the value of career planning.

We want your child to know that it's okay not to know what they want to do. It's also okay to change jobs/careers if and when you figure out that you made a choice that wasn't exactly the best for you.

In New Zealand the labour market is highly dynamic. Every year 200,000 jobs are created and 150,000 destroyed. The average person will go through 12 jobs and four career changes in their lifetime (source *www.careers.govt.nz).*

Globalisation and technological change means to succeed, job seekers have to be flexible, learn new skills, and be very responsive to labour market trends.

How to teach your child this important lesson

Get your child to think of a career, (write it down) then have him go through the following questions and explore the answers.

When making a decision about a career it is important that it is the individuals decision and they are not pressured from others such as family or friends.

Consider these points as you discuss their options

What excites you about this occupation or career?

What type of education and training will you need?

Where will you get the training and skills you need?

What is the earning potential of this type of career?

Could you see this job becoming redundant or obsolete?

What do I enjoy doing – could I make a career from this?

If your child chooses a career path that you may not have chosen, encourage them to explore all the avenues that it offers.

Silbo says

- **Any idea is a good idea**
- **Everything ever made started with an idea**

When you think of all the things in the world you start to realise that somebody, somewhere, had an idea. The electric light bulb, the telephone all started with just an idea that someone thought of.

Sometimes ideas for making money come naturally and other times it helps to brainstorm with a group of people to help get the creative juices flowing. Thinking about what ideas you can come up with will start you thinking of ways and possibilities of earning extra money.

How to teach your child this important lesson

Get your child to look at one room in your house and examine everything in detail so he can see how many ideas people had to create for what they see now. It can be a fun activity to do with the whole family by asking everyone if they can come up with improvements of things that have been created already or if any one has an inspiration for a new idea.

Tell the story of how in April 2008 news broke of two young New Zealander computer programmers, Guy Horrocks and Layton Duncan. They saw an opportunity with the new Apple iphone. They noticed two features missing, one being a search function, so they wrote a programme which could be added to the iphone. By early 2008 over 400,000 copies had been downloaded at $10.00 per copy, which meant a turnover of $4,000,000. Yes, four million dollars.

Share with your child the types of things that you did as a child to earn money. You could look on the internet for ideas for jobs for kids.

Get together with your child and brainstorm to see what you can dream up in the way of ideas to make some money during their next holidays and weekends.

What do you need to do to make this happen?

- **Think about how many hours you have to work to pay for something**

This page is designed to help your child think about how many hours they or you (their parents) have had to work to pay for a "need" or "want". Many adults are working long hours to provide needs and wants for their families without taking the time to stop and think about what they are doing and why they are doing it! Is the time you spend at work worth sacrificing the time you could spend with your family at home, or saving that extra for long-term financial freedom? For example, if a person earns $12.00 per hour after tax and their car payment is $80.00 per week – they have to work 6.6 hours (or nearly a full day) every week just to pay for their car payment. A person who earns $20.00 per hour after tax needs to work 4 hours (half a day) per week just to pay for their car payment.

Many adults have never broken down the costs of things into how many hours they have had to work for that money to buy a particular "need" or "want". The understanding of this concept should help your child to evaluate if spending their money on that "need or want" was worth the number of hours worked to get it. It will also help them appreciate how many hours you have had to work to pay for things they take for granted around their home such as food, clothes, housing, car, TV etc.

How to teach your child this important lesson

Look at each item on the list and work out how many hours have to be worked to buy that particular "want" and "need" to get the idea of how it works. Then think of some things you have bought recently and work out how many hours you have had to work to pay for them. Simply divide the cost of the goods by your net hourly rate. It can be a great question to ask your child or yourself when considering any purchase, especially large ones, "How many hours will I have to work to pay for this?"

Work out things like your monthly electricity bill and see how many hours you have had to work to pay for that.

> **"Never become so much of an expert that you stop gaining expertise. View life as a continuous learning experience."**
> **Denis Waitley**

	Cost per week $	Amount earned per hour after tax			
		$11.00	$15.00	$17.00	$22.00
		Number of hours of work needed to pay for things			
Food	180.00	16 hr 22 min	12 hr 00 min	10 hr 35 min	08 hr 11 min
Clothing	20.00	01 hr 49 min	01 hr 20 min	01 hr 11 min	00 hr 55 min
Housing	240.00	21 hr 49 min	16 hr 00 min	14 hr 07 min	10 hr 55 min
Car payment	50.00	04 hr 33 min	03 hr 20 min	02 hr 56 min	02 hr 16 min
Petrol	40.00	03 hr 38 min	02 hr 40 min	02 hr 21 min	01 hr 49 min
Power	35.00	03 hr 11 min	02 hr 20 min	02 hr 04 min	01 hr 35 min
TOTAL		**51.36 Hrs**	**37.67 Hrs**	**33.24 Hrs**	**25.68 Hrs**

Take note of how many fewer hours per week you would have to work if you earn a higher dollar rate per hour

Now let's look at some bigger items that you might buy for yourself

	Cost of item $	Amount earned per hour after tax			
		$11.00	$15.00	$17.00	$22.00
		Number of hours of work needed to pay for things			
Car	23,000.00	2090 hr 55 min	1533 hr 20 min	1352 hr 56 min	1045 hours
Car	6,500.00	590 hr 55 min	433 hr 20 min	382 hr 21 min	295 hours
Big TV	3,520.00	320 hr 00 min	234 hr 40 min	207 hr 04 min	160 hours
Computer	2,400.00	218 hr 11 min	160 hr 00 min	141 hr 11 min	109 hours
Lounge Suite	1,750.00	159 hr 05 min	116 hr 40 min	102 hr 56 min	79 hours
Stereo	840.00	76 hr 22 min	56 hr 00 min	49 hr 25 min	38 hours

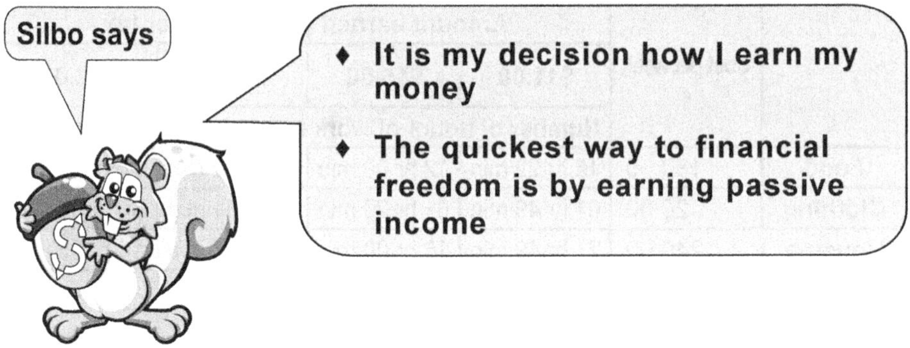

Though there are two types of income. Active income (working hours for dollars) and Passive income (money you can earn without having a "job").

From these two types of income there are four ways to wealth. None of them is the right or wrong way, it is just a matter of choosing which one is right for you.

Active

1. Being an employee.
2. As a self-employed person.

Passive

3. Business activities (such as rental income).
4. Portfolio income such as dividends, interest, capital gains and royalties.

Sometimes when people decide to leave their jobs and become self employed (or buy a business), they become disillusioned because they didn't realise they still have to work hours for dollars. But now, no work, no pay! They have just bought themselves a job. However, one of the advantages of being self employed is they can deduct many expenses such as a portion of running their car as a legitimate business expense, which reduces the amount of tax they have to pay.

Get to know what source your income comes from - either trading hours for dollars or from passive income. This will help you assess what could be a better investment in the longer term. If you don't create any passive income it is very difficult to ever be free to choose what you want to do with your time. Being financially independent gives you choices so you can follow your dreams – whether it be working voluntarily for some cause you are passionate about or caring for your grandchildren, or travelling for an extended length of time if you wish to.

When you are deciding about which career path you may wish to follow, consider whether it will always be a job you will have to work hours for dollars or will there be an opportunity in the future to earn passive income. Some jobs or businesses may lead you to being able to earn passive income quicker than others.

How to teach your child this important lesson

The following are three different activities that will help reinforce the idea of active and passive income.

ACTIVITY ONE:

Have your child think of a job or business. Then get him to decide if the income he could earn will be active income (1) or (2). Or will it be passive income by (3) or (4).

Active Income

1. Working for a boss
2. Own your own business but still have to work in it

Passive Income

3. Rental property
4. Portfolio income earned from shares or bonds, dividends and royalties

Use the following questions to help decide which income category that job or business would fall under.

1. Who employs you?
2. How are you paid (hourly, salary, commission, interest, appreciation)?
3. When and how much do you work (8, 10 or 12 hours a day, weekends, etc.)?
4. What skills, knowledge and training do you need?
5. What are your responsibilities?
6. Who pays your superannuation?
7. Who takes the risks?
8. Who controls how much money you can make?
9. Can you deduct expenses from your wages?
10. Who controls when you take your holidays, sick leave, and time off?

Most people start off their working life in the "employed" section where they gain experience and then perhaps branch out into being self employed etc. An employed person who saves regularly can very quickly get into the "passive income category" by receiving interest on what they have in the bank.

There is NO wrong place to be. The right place to be is the place that brings you pleasure and gives you a sense of satisfaction!

How to teach your child this important lesson

ACTIVITY TWO

Simply read the story of John the plumber. Get your child to identify the passive income which Silbo says is the quickest road to being and staying financially well. Discuss the two different types of income and follow the path of how John progresses firstly from being employed, then self employed, then he employs others, and finally no longer needs to work.

Have your child ask family and friend's parents about the different types of income they create and how they create it. If you feel uncomfortable about this, it is probably because of a belief you have about this. A good way is to let your child be innocent and learn from other's decisions and choices.

1 Active Income

John owns his own plumbing business.

He is self employed. He still works hours for dollars.

If he doesn't work he doesn't get paid.

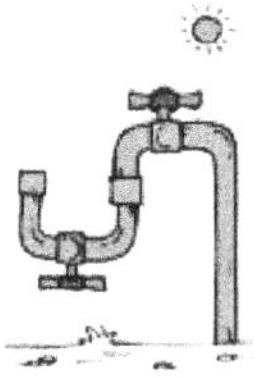

2 John pays Fred and Bill to work in his business. John still does some plumbing work and makes sure there is plenty of work for them to do so he can pay their wages.

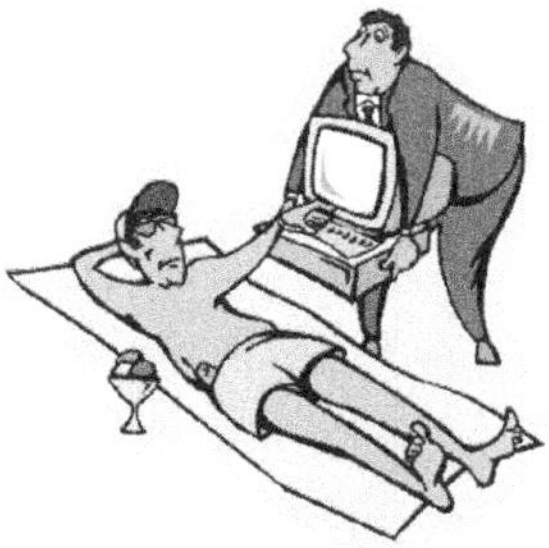

3 Passive Income

After a while John's business is so successful he can employ a person to manage his business and so he no longer needs to go to work. Instead he gets a share of the profit every month.

4 He has also bought a property which he gets paid rent for plus he has bought some shares in another company which he gets paid some dividends every 12 months.

Would you rather be John in 1 and 2, or 3 and 4?

Do you think John was on the road to financial security in number 3?

What are some other examples of Active and Passive Income?

How to teach your child this important lesson

ACTIVITY THREE

Get your child to go through each occupation and tick which category (active or passive) income the occupation fits into, keeping in mind that sometimes it could be more than one.

Discuss with your child which income category (active or passive) that you fit into. Also get him to consider the job that he is considering doing. Ask him what category he thinks this would fit into.

OCCUPATION	ACTIVE INCOME	PASSIVE INCOME
Electrician		
Jims lawn-mowing		
KFC owner		
Nurse		
Builder		
Bus driver		
Receptionist		
Landlord		
Teacher		
Astronaut		
Sky diver instructor		
Dentist		
Property developer		
Share trader		
Property investor		
Doctor		

- **Save 10% of everything you earn**
- **Make saving a habit**
- **It takes 21 days to establish a habit**

A habit is described in the dictionary as a regularly repeated behaviour pattern. An action or pattern of behaviour that is repeated so often that it becomes typical of somebody, although he or she may be unaware of it. As we know, there can be Smart habits and there can be Dumb habits. If we regularly do not save, then we have a dumb habit that needs to be changed.

To save a little of everything you earn is one of the oldest and most effective money principles in existence. Your child might not see startling results when they begin their saving. No matter how small the amount, train them to put a small bit aside as soon as they get it and before they even consider what they want to use the rest for. The habit of saving the first 10% before anything else is what will help them on their way to financial wellness.

How to teach your child this important lesson

If he doesn't have one already, take your child to the bank and open a savings account. You could get him to ask the bank some questions to make sure he is getting the best interest for his money.

Such as

How much money do I need to open an account?

How much interest do you pay?

When is the interest added to my account?

What are the fees you will charge me?

Is there a fee if I withdraw my money?

See if you can come up with some more questions.

Go to more than one bank to see who offers the best deals.

Once the account is set up, make a time once a month (or week) to go and put a portion of what he has earned into his savings account. If you do this as a habit he will be amazed at how fast it builds up.

Have your child think of some examples of some positive habits that will lead to financial wellness and some habits that will lead to being financially sick.

Some supermarkets have a policy that if the price on the shelf is lower than what comes out on the docket then the amount of that item will be given to you free! The smart habit to be learned here is to always check your dockets.

Share with your child your own money habits, good and bad and how they have affected your life, your relationships and your financial success.

Look at these habits and see how they could be smart or dumb.

Smart Habits		Dumb Habits
Get up when the alarm goes off		Stay in bed when the alarm goes off
Always check your shopping docket to see you got charged the right amount		Don't bother to check your shopping docket to see if you got charged the right amount
Always check your change		Don't bother to check your change
	You think of a habit that could be smart or dumb	

Now think of some other habits that help you become financially well or financially sick.

- **A million dollars obtained from a windfall doesn't mean you will always stay a millionaire**

Money that comes from not working for it (easy money) usually comes from an inheritance or luck, such as winning the lottery. The track record of people who get their money through the lottery or other windfalls is usually very different from those who created their wealth themselves or who planned for an expected inheritance. Some lottery winners are often a sorry lot. More than 90 percent use up their winnings within 10 years – some go through their money in weeks or months.

You must understand that just because you are given a million dollars you may not always stay a millionaire (unless you have developed good habits and a healthy relationship with money).

How to teach your child this important lesson

Have your child read 1- 5 of the following habits of millionaires out loud and have a conversation about each one.

Five habits of Millionaires (adapted from www.career-advice.monster.com) are:

1) Avoid the earn-to-spend mentality.
2) Focus on what they want.
3) Do whatever is necessary to meet their goal.
4) Take calculated risks.
5) Are generous.

These five habits are a pretty good prescription for living happily even if you're not a millionaire!

My husband and I owned a small grocery store. An observation we made was that people who were struggling financially were generally those that regularly spent their money on non essentials such as lottery tickets, junk food, fizzy drinks and cigarettes. Although we gained from them being our customers, they would have been better off financially spending their money at a big supermarket where prices were much cheaper. Our more financially successful customers didn't purchase those items on a regular basis.

People who are working towards being financially free invest in assets instead of buying "stuff".

- **Leverage can be a good way to create wealth**
- **Work smarter not harder**

Using other people's money, time and energy is called leverage. It is when you use the banks money to buy an investment property. It is when you get 10 people working and earning money for your business instead of doing the job alone. It can also be when you have an investment property and have a tenant paying off the mortgage.

It is good to learn the principle of leverage early so that your children are learning to work smarter instead of harder (not that hard work is wrong). The idea is to maximise the earning potential from any given situation. That may mean employing the help of others to work in a business or to get a job done quickly.

How to teach your child this important lesson

Ask your child how he would lift a large rock if no one was around to help. You could set up a physical form of a lever system where he has to lift something that is too heavy to lift by himself but with the help of a pole propped on top of a box he could lift it easily. Explain this is called leverage. Ask him to think about a see saw in a playground and see if he can explain why a heavy person can balance with a lighter person. Using leverage increases your capabilities of what you can do by yourself.

So, do you think you could move something that is bigger and heavier than you? Yes of course you can, you just need some leverage! The same goes for making money, sometimes you just need some leverage (maybe some money from the bank or other investors). Ask your child to think how he could take advantage of leverage to make money. You could share any experiences you have had with using leverage to make you money.

Leverage means using

Other people's time

Other people's energy

Other people's money

- **Know how to work out how much profit you make**
- **Lack of knowledge can trip you up**

It is important to know exactly how much profit you make when you sell something. Many people think when they buy something and then sell it for more than they paid for it that the difference between the two amounts is the profit.

How much you sell something for must have expenses (including tax you will have to pay) deducted from it to come up with the real amount of profit you make.

Many times children do not understand this concept, because Mum or Dad may not have charged them interest for money that is borrowed or for the cost of petrol if they are helping their child deliver pamphlets for example.

They also need to know the difference between pre-tax profit (profit before tax is paid) and after-tax profit (profit after tax is paid). After tax profit is the "real profit" you have to spend.

Be careful about what you say around your child when talking about how much profit you have made from something. For example if you say you bought a house for $100,000 and you sold it for $150,000 so you made $50,00 profit but forget to mention you had to re paint it, carpet it plus the cost of interest you borrowed, then your child is getting a false impression of what profit actually is. Many adults are quick to make it sound like they have made huge profits from something but the truth of it is they didn't mention what it actually cost them to make the sale.

How to teach your child this important lesson

Go through these two examples with your child. Pretend your child is going to deliver pamphlets and plans to buy a bike and sell it at a profit.

If your child tries his hand at buying or selling something and doesn't make a profit due to lack of experience then sometimes the best money lesson for life would be to let them make a loss and to owe you the money. They will be much more careful the next time.

Example 1

Income from pamphlet delivery		$20.00
Expenses		
Petrol for Mums car	$5.00	
Rubber bands	.50	
Carry bag	$2.00	
	$7.50	
	=====	
Pre-tax Gross income (Income – Expenses)		$ 12.50
Tax (estimate 20% tax)	$ 2.50	
	=====	
Real income after tax is deducted (Net income)		**$10.00**
		======

Example 2

Your child buys a bike really cheaply for $20.00 which needs new brakes and a new tyre. They think they can sell it for a profit of $30.00.

They find they can only sell it for $30.00.

It is good to teach your child to get an accurate cost of what it is going to cost to fix it before they buy it.

Income from sale of bike		$30.00
Cost of Bike	$20.00	
Expenses		
Brakes	$ 2.00	
Bike tyre	$10.00	
		$32.00
		=====
Pre-tax profit or loss is income less expenses		($ 2.00)
Tax (in this case there is no tax because he made a loss)		$ 00.00
		=====
Real profit (loss) after tax is deducted		**($2.00)**
		======

Silbo says

- **Work six days and rest one day**
- **Keep your work/life in balance**
- **Making more money is not always the answer. It is what you do with it that matters**

It is important to have one day in the week where you rest and do not work. Plan what you are going to do on your rest day ahead of time so you are refreshed, ready to start the working week again. The "Wheel of Life" is a way of reminding yourself that you need to allocate time to other things instead of work. Your child needs to learn that it is important to have time for rest – just to do things they want to do – not to have every minute of their day programmed.

If you are one of those people who are "go getters" and are goal orientated, you run the risk of being successful in your working career but have other areas such as your family and your health falling apart around you. Many people do not take into account other areas of their life apart from working. It is often only when a crisis happens in your health or family that you are forced to look at how you are living your life. If children have parents who model a life that is out of balance, then there is more probability your child will grow up and be more susceptible to being burnt out physically, mentally and emotionally.

How to teach your child this important lesson

Complete the questionnaire on the next page with your child. You can either fill it in for yourself with the help of your child or help him fill it in for himself. Beware he may be very honest! However, it can be a good way to help discover if your child thinks you have a good work/life balance. Then mark your score on the diagram along the line for each area. A score of 10 is put on the outer circle line. A score of 5 is somewhere in the middle and a score of 1 will be in the centre circle. Then join the dots and get a graphic overview of the areas in your life which are in balance and those that are out of balance. We suggest that if you discover areas of your life or your child's life that are way out of balance then you take the lowest score first and decide to make some changes.

WHEEL OF LIFE QUESTIONNAIRE

Name______________________________Date __________________________

1. Tick each box where you can answer yes to the question. Score yourself out of 10 for each section. If the question does not apply to you - leave blank and change the score to out of 9 or 8. This will particularly apply to some of the adult type questions such as about work etc.
2. Mark your score on the circle diagram along the line for each area. Join the dots and get a graphic overview of the balance of your life. I suggest you start looking at the area of your life in which you scored the lowest first.

Physical & Health — Score/10

1	My body weight is in proportion to my height and frame	
2	I ensure that I get adequate regular physical exercise	
3	I get adequate sleep and wake refreshed	
4	I am free of habits that endanger my health	
5	I have good general health	
6	I pay attention to my personal hygiene	
7	I am aware of my physical needs and meet them	
8	My school/work environment is easy and relaxing to be in	
9	I enjoy time in nature and harmonious environments	
10	My diet is balanced and healthy with adequate fresh food	

Career & Financial — Score /10

1	I have specific plans for the development of my career	
2	I am happy and passionate about my work	
3	I enjoy a good work/life balance	
4	I effectively manage work related stress	
5	My career allows me to fulfil my creative talents and abilities	
6	My income allows me to live the life I want	
7	Generally, I live within my income	
8	I have an active plan for financial growth	
9	I use credit responsibly	
10	I behave financially ethically	

Family & Home — Score /10

1	I have open and honest communication with all members of my family	
2	I have a partner/spouse with whom I have a stable healthy relationship	
3	I regularly spend quality time with each family member where I am able	
4	My family feel they can come to me with any problems and vice versa	
5	My partner and I regularly plan time together	
6	My relationship with my partner is mutually supportive	
7	I enjoy a good level of intimacy with my partner	
8	My home environment is peaceful and harmonious	
9	I look forward to coming home after work	
10	I have an area of my home either inside or outside that I enjoy	

Mental & Educational

Score /10

1	Generally I have a positive attitude	
2	I am aware of my strengths and weaknesses	
3	I can adapt my emotional state when appropriate	
4	I am committed to my own mental/emotional fitness	
5	I enjoy a wide range of interests and activities	
6	I am actively involved in some study that will advance my goals	
7	I am inquisitive and regularly learn new things	
8	I read literature that is informative and broadens my horizons	
9	I am aware of the most recent trends that are applicable to my life	
10	My education level supports me in attaining my personal goals	

Social & Recreation

Score /10

1	I have a strong varied network of friends	
2	As a whole, people trust me and value my opinion	
3	I find it easy to relax and enjoy myself in company	
4	I find it easy to relate to members of both sexes	
5	I enjoy a range of interests that keep me healthy and energised	
6	I have adequate time off work to pursue my interests	
7	I participate in the social and cultural life of my community	
8	I have boundaries with my friends where we all feel respected	
9	I have friends I can call on when I need help	
10	I find it easy to relate to people from different ethnic or socio-economic backgrounds	

Spiritual & Ethical

Score /10

1	I live my life in integrity according to a clear set of values	
2	I treat others as I want to be treated	
3	I have a strong sense of purpose in life	
4	I nurture my spiritual beliefs and allow others to do the same	
5	I live with a clear conscience	
6	I feel that I belong to life and that life supports me	
7	I regularly engage in some activity that connects me to my God	
8	I read inspirational literature regularly	
9	My beliefs about life are able to support me during tough times	
10	I associate with people who help me to live according to my spiritual beliefs and values	

WHEEL OF LIFE

(Keep it in balance)

Mark your score on the diagram along the line for each area. A score of 10 is put on the outer circle line. A score of 5 is somewhere in the middle and a score of 1 will be in the centre circle. Then join the dots and get a graphic overview of the areas in your life which are in balance and those that are out of balance.

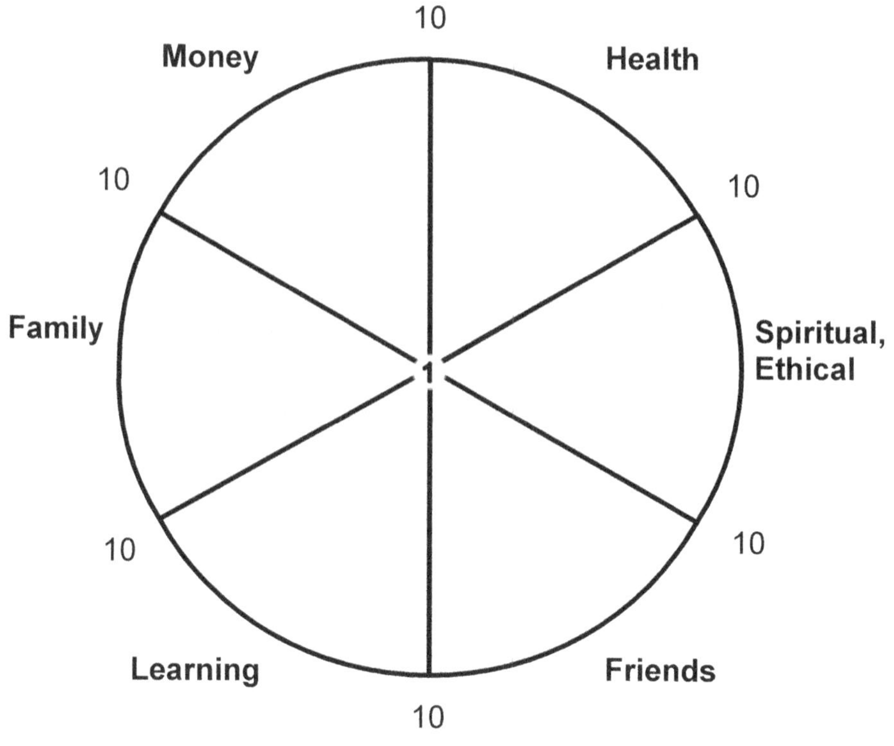

"Be aware of wonder. Live a balanced life - learn some and think some and draw and paint and sing and dance and play and work every day some."
<u>Robert Fulghum</u>

NOTES

Step 5

> **"For knowledge itself is power."**
>
> **Francis Bacon**

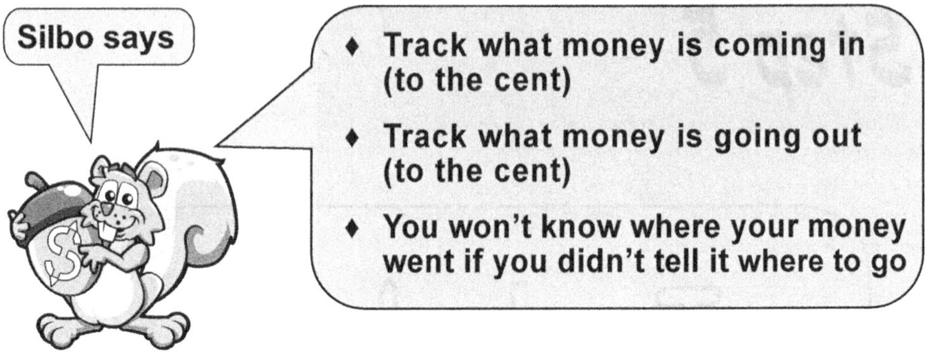

To know what money is coming in and what is going out you need to have a plan. "It is better to tell your money where to go instead of wondering where it has gone". This is called tracking. Keeping a written record of your spending will automatically reduce your spending. When I was trying to lose weight I was told I would lose it faster when I wrote down every bit of food and drink that passed my mouth (and it was true). It is the same with spending, if you write down every single thing you spend your money on and ask yourself "why did I spend that money?" You will become more aware of where your money is going and make better choices.

For you to reach financial freedom in the future, you need to make conscious choices with your money instead of buying things on a "whim". You need to know what you are doing with your money so that it doesn't disappear without a trace. It is also important for you and your child to think about what emotion is triggered by buying a particular purchase. Think about your thinking and the feeling you get when you purchase something. If you are buying something to meet an emotional need or to impress someone else, then you are destroying valuable money seeds. Thinking about what you are spending and why you are spending it is the first step towards making positive change.

How to teach your child this important lesson

There are two ways to teach your child how to start tracking. One way is to give your child an allocated amount of cash (this works best for this exercise). Ask your child to keep track of how he spends that allocated amount of money over the week. Get him to ask for receipts to prove where he spent the money. The second way is to get him to help you record for a week what you have spent your money on. Get receipts for everything to prove your spending. Again, cash works best for this exercise as when the cash is gone, it is gone and it is easy to see where you have missed tracking your expenses. You may be surprised at what you spend your money on.

This is a great activity to do with the whole family. You could offer a prize for those who are able to account for every cent they have spent at the end of the week and have receipts to prove it. To make it easier to track, decorate a box where all receipts are to be kept, then it is just a matter of writing down on a page in separate columns for each type of spending. At the end of doing that you will see clearly where your money is going.

Use the table below to track what happens to your money over the next week. Deduct or add to the balance each time you make a transaction. Photocopy this page or use a small notebook to carry around with you so have it with you where ever you go. I know you can do it – it is easy when you know how.

DATE	Description and reason for purchase	Income	Expense	Balance
			Starting balance	$

The first step to being in control of your money instead of it controlling you, is knowing where your money goes.

- **Healthy money habits will put you on the path to financial freedom**
- **Use the Triple S P system for handling all your money**

The money jars are a simple but highly effective way to take control of your money. Teaching your child to use the Triple S P system early on in their life will create a habit that will set them on the road to knowing exactly where their money is going. We have called our system the SSSP system (triple S P system) where we have three jars (Sharing, Saving and Spending) for our income to go into. From these three jars money is distributed as necessary by using a written plan. This is the "P" part of the system.

Having your child learn this simple concept of telling their money where to go instead of wondering where it's gone helps create a great money habit that will eventually lead to financial prosperity. It is important for your child to actually "handle money" to see how it feels, to see it build up and what it feels like when it is all spent.

Caution – Be careful not to "rescue" your child if they have spent all their money and want to buy something else. That can be a very valuable lesson – when the jar is empty, it is empty! Letting your child borrow from you until next pay day is only teaching them to spend more than they earn. This can have serious consequences in the future when they are old enough to take out loans.

How to teach your child this important lesson

Use the words on the next page to explain the Triple S P System, using Money Jars as an example. Have your child create his own set of jars. (Sharing, Saving, and Spending). Be sure to use jars that are see-through glass or plastic so your child can see the money accumulating. We suggest that you get them to put "real coins or paper money" into the money jar for a start. As soon as an agreed amount is reached, take your child to the bank and put it into an account for safe keeping. Then you could use a sticker to write on the amount that is now in their bank account. Another option would be to use a marble to represent each dollar, or say $10.00 so your child has a feeling that they can still "see" their money. If you are able to purchase plastic play money, this could be an excellent alternative to real money. Avoid the temptation of putting the money into the bank for them, and using an Eftpos card. Children need to learn by seeing, doing and touching the money for themselves.

Parental challenge: Set up three bank accounts (or jars with labels) and use the Triple S P system for yourself. This can be another great way to show your child how to manage money and at the same time learn for yourself.

The Money Jars

Your money has three different jobs. Sharing it with others, Saving for the future, and Spending it on needs and wants. Putting your money into named jars indicates where you want it to go. If you don't tell your money where to go you will wonder where it's gone! Has that ever happened to you? " I wonder where that money went?" Information received from the NZ Department of Statistics in April 2008 tells us that for every $1 New Zealanders make, they spend $1.14. False prosperity is owning things bought on credit. Overspending will cause you to become financially sick. "It won't happen overnight – but it will happen!"

Wisemoney.co.nz sell money jars called 'moon jars' which you can order on-line.

Jar 1 is your Sharing Jar

Silbo says "Think of others first and give away a percentage of your income". There is a Universal Law (you reap what you sow) that works like this: if you give something away, it comes back to you multiplied. It may not come back to you in the exact form you gave it, but rest assured if you sow goodness it will be returned to you. Sharing can be done in many ways and could be in the form of a donation to your favourite charity, support a child in a third world country, church, helping a neighbour to buy groceries or paying for someone else to attend a special event. Another principle is if you look after what you have then you are more likely to receive more.

Jar 2 is your Savings Jar

You can divide this jar into two basic categories, short-term savings and long-term savings. Whether you use two separate jars or two bank accounts, it is good to keep big object savings or long-term savings, (eg new house or investment) separate from short term savings such as a new bike, a special family outing, holiday, new car or "JIC money" (just in case money). Think about what it would be like to have three or six months of living expenses in a separate bank account. This would buy you some time if you needed to reassess where you were going in life or where you wanted to go.

Jar 3 is your Spending Jar

This jar is for all your living expenses and covers all your "needs" and all your "wants". From needs such as food, shelter and clothing, electricity etc to wants such as takeaways and a new stereo. It is important to know how much you are spending in each area of your life so you can then allocate the appropriate money to cover that expense. "Knowing your expenses" is covered later in this lesson along with showing you how to draw up a SSSP that will make it easy for you to keep track of where your money is going!

Distribute your weekly income into your money jars (or separate bank accounts).

SHARING

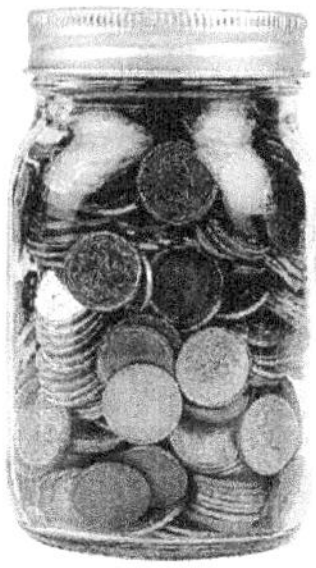

10%

Sponsor a child in a third world country

Church donations

Help people in need

Support a friend

Support a charity

Donation to worthy causes such as Red Cross, Tear Fund or Ruel Foundation

SAVING

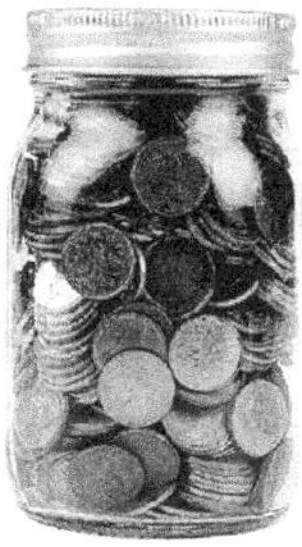

10%

Short Term Saving

Family holiday

New car

New lawn mower

"Just in case" money

Long Term Saving

New home

Retirement

Investment

Kids' tertiary studies

SPENDING

80%

Food
Petrol
School lunches
Internet
Power
Insurances
Rent/Mortgage
Car repairs
New clothes
Car registration/WOF
Rates
Doctor/ Chemist
Telephone/cell phone

TELL YOUR MONEY WHERE TO GO INSTEAD OF WONDERING WHERE IT'S GONE!

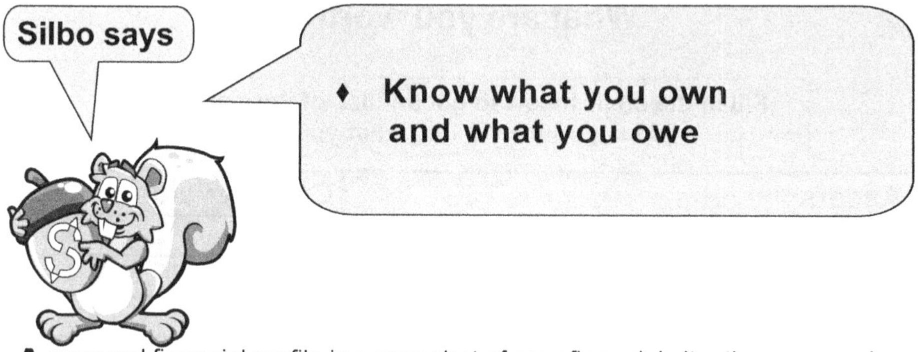

A personal financial profile is a snapshot of your financial situation on any given day and it changes from day to day, month to month, year to year. It is common practice for a lending institution to ask for a statement of assets and liabilities to determine if you have sufficient funds or assets should you have trouble making your repayments. Your net worth is what you own minus what you owe. This gives you a place to start when making future financial decisions.

You need to keep constant tabs on how well you are doing financially, otherwise you won't know when to buy or sell certain investments to keep your money working as hard for you as you can.

When financial institutions are determining whether they think you are a good financial risk or not, they won't look at how many degrees you have, if you passed maths or not, all they look at is your financial history. You may think that you are a fantastic credit risk because you earn a huge salary. However, if you already have huge outgoings to match your huge salary and owe more than you own, then it is likely you will be refused credit. They look at things like how much have you saved, previous credit history, what you own, monthly outgoings etc.

How to teach your child this important lesson

The best way to do this page is to talk about your own assets and liabilities statement with your child so he can do the exercise with real figures. If you don't want to do that for some reason, then help him to do a net worth for himself. Find out what he owns and what he owes. When valuing things in the home that your child may own because it was given as a birthday present, make sure he puts the value down of what it could sell for now, not what it cost. Make sure you put down anything that your child might owe (such as he borrowed a dollar from you and hasn't paid it back).

Note: For this activity we have used how financial institutions view assets and liabilities. They generally view an asset as something you have that they could sell to get some money. However, Robert Kiyosaki in his book "Rich Dad, Poor Dad" views a liability as anything that is not producing an income, which in some ways is a more correct way of looking at "stuff". This is because if you have "stuff" sitting around the house you are not using which could be sold and that money used for saving and receiving interest from it, then it is definitely a liability! This can be a great activity for the whole family to do individually. It could be a good wake up call for any members of your family who have lots of consumer debt.

What are you worth?

Fill in the chart below to get an idea of your net worth (what you own minus what your owe).

Assets	**Current value $**
Cash in (bank accounts)	
Money in retirement account	
Family home	
Cars owned	
Investment property owned	
Shares owned	
Bonus Bonds owned	
Mutual Funds owned	
Money people owe you	
Jewellery	
Stereo	
Other assets/investments	
TOTAL ASSETS	$

Liabilities	**Current value $**
Unsecured bank loans (bank overdraft)	
Secured bank loans	
Car loan	
Mortgages (home loan)	
Credit card debt	
Store cards	
Unpaid bills	
Hire purchases	
TOTAL LIABILITIES	$
Your net worth	**$**
(Total assets minus total liabilities)	

Silbo says

- **It is important how to know how to read a pay slip**
- **Net income is income received after all expenses are deducted**

It is important to understand how to read a pay slip so you know how much you are earning and what is being taken out of your pay before you receive it. Many children do not understand that when they start working the Government requires them to take tax out of their wages before they get it. They also fund education, medical and hospital services, public roads, police, the courts and justice systems, the armed forces and sickness and unemployment benefits. Your taxes help pay for the things that make our New Zealand culture happen. Such as by funding agencies like Creative NZ and NZ on Air, which pay for NZ music videos, bands and theatre.

In general children aren't shown their parents pay slip and also mum and dad don't take taxes out of their pocket money! So the first time they get paid from a job they can be shocked when they see that they didn't get all their gross income, but a net income (gross income minus taxes). Learning about taxes and other deductions (such as clothing allowances, superannuation and student loans prepares them for understanding their first pay slip and knowing exactly what is being taken out before they get their final pay and why. It is also important to understand their pay slip so they can work out if they have been paid the correct amount or not and that the employer sends tax to the Government on their behalf.

How to teach your child this important lesson

Simply go through the sample pay slip on the next page and help him answer the questions. Explain the terms Gross Income (income before tax) and Net Income (income received after taxes) and YTD (year to date) (income or taxes earned or paid so far this financial year).This pay slip is for the first pay period of the financial year. Note that the pay period ends on the 16 April but Samantha doesn't actually get paid until the 20th April. This is to allow time for the pay clerk to process the pays. Samantha is employed for 40 hrs per week but this week had a public holiday (stat leave) so she was paid for 8 hours even though she didn't have to go to work. Explain to your child that when he starts work, most times he will have to complete a time sheet so the employer knows how much to pay him. No pay sheet – no pay. When you are training your child to do extra work round the house, you could make up a sheet they have to record how much time he "works" for you to get in practice for the real world.

Show your child a copy of your pay slip and answer the same questions. Inform your child that when you work for someone else (trade your time for money), you pay taxes first. When you are self-employed, own a business or are an investor, you pay taxes after deducting all your expenses from your income.

Pay advice

Handy Andy's Appliances Fendon Street Branch Samantha Silbo Tax number: 12 345 67				Pay date 20/04/09 Pay period 02/04/09- 16/04/09	
Earnings	Hours	**Rate per hour**	**Amount**	**Deductions**	
Ordinary Hrs	32	10.00	320.00	PAYE	68.16
Overtime	0.5	10.00	5.00	SUPER	16.80
Stat Leave	8	10.00	80.00		
Total gross income			**405.00**	**Total deductions**	**84.96**
Year To Date					
Gross Pay		405.00		Gross Pay	405.00
Deductions		84.96		Deductions	84.96
Net Pay		320.04		**Net Pay**	**320.04**
Employee Super Payments		$16.80			
Employer Super Contribution		$16.80	Employer Super Contribution $16.80		
Deposited to bank account : 06 0413 01234 00					**$320.04**

YTD = Year to Date, Super = Superannuation, PAYE = Pay as you earn Tax

Try answering these questions

How often does Samantha get paid?	
How much did Samantha earn per hour?	
What was her gross income?	
How much tax has she paid this year?	
Who is Samantha's employer?	
How many hours did she work?	
How much did she get for overtime?	
What was her net income?	
How much superannuation has Samantha's employer contributed this year?	

Remember that when you work for someone else you pay taxes first!

When you are self-employed, own a business or are an investor, you pay taxes after deducting all your expenses from your income!

- **You need to know how to read and understand a bank statement**
- **A bank statement should be used to confirm your money has done what you told it to do**

A paper account statement from the bank can show how money has entered and left your life over the last month or week depending on how often you ask your bank to send you statements. Many people do most of their banking over the internet and can access a copy of their bank statement on-line which gives an up to date picture of what has been happening to their money.

It is important for children to understand the different ways of paying for things such as direct debits, automatic payments, Eftpos, withdrawing cash from the automatic teller machine and how these are recorded on a bank statement. It is also important that they learn how to read their bank statement and check that money has gone in and out of their account as it should have. Many people think that banks must be correct, however from personal experience this is not always the case. A bank statement should be used to confirm that your money has done what you told it to do, not the other way around, of using your bank account statement to see where your money went.

How to teach your child this important lesson

Read the bank statement below and on the following page as a "story" of what has happened in the financial life of the Silbo family during the end of April 2008 and the month of May 2008. See if your child can spot where you are up to in the story by following along with the bank statement.

On the 29th April 2008 Simon and Samantha Silbo started with a credit balance of $246.48 in the bank with bank account number 38 9010 9302204-02. The first two digits of their account number (38) tells us that they have an account with Kiwi Bank and the next four numbers (9010) tell us the branch at which the account is held. The next lot of numbers (9302204) tell us what the account number is and the final two numbers (02) (suffix numbers) tell us what type of account it is (whether it is a savings account, everyday account or loan account). This is Simon and Samantha's account they use for amounts they have allocated for spending. They have three other bank accounts with Kiwi Bank under the same account number. Their Sharing account ends with an -01 and their Savings account ends with an -03 and finally the loan they have for their mortgage ends with -05.

Simon works for a Computer Company called ITEC and is paid weekly. On 29th April ITEC Computer Services direct credit Simon's wages of $600.00 which increases their bank balance to $846.48. On 30th April the bank takes out their monthly fee of $5.00 for running their account which reduces their bank balance to $841.48.

On the 1st of May, Samantha using internet banking transfers $60.00 into their account number 9302204-01 for sharing with others and then $60.00 into their account number 9302204-03 for saving. This reduces their bank balance to $721.48.

On the 1st of every month they top up their cell phone with $10.00 so they can text friends and family. Simon used his Eftpos (POS) card number 23443259648 which is unique to him. Samantha also has an Eftpos (POS) number 23443259649 which is unique to her. This is so they know who has made a particular withdrawal from their account. To use their cards they have to use a PIN (personal identification number) to protect them against someone else using their card. The $10.00 purchase to top up their cell phone reduced their bank balance to $711.48. Eftpos cards can also be known as debit cards. Which means when you use a "debit card" it takes money out of your bank account.

On the 1st May they withdrew $250.00 cash from the ATM (automatic teller machine) in Springfield. They use this cash to put petrol of $80.00 into their car, $150.00 for food and $20.00 for treats. They don't use their Eftpos card any more that week because all their income is planned in the way they want to spend it. This reduces their bank balance to $461.48.

On the 3rd May Slingshot uses a Direct Debit of $83.00 (an arrangement by which sums of money of varying amounts that are owed at regular intervals are paid directly from your bank account) to pay for their telephone and broadband connection and the tolls they used for the previous month. This reduces their bank balance to $378.48.

On the 3rd May using internet banking, Simon pays for the annual Contents Insurance bill of $283.22 that they have for their household possessions using the "Bill Payment" facility. This reduces their bank balance to $95.26.

On the 6th May ITEC Computer Services direct credit Simon's wages of $600.00 which increases their bank balance to $695.26.

So that Simon and Samantha don't forget to pay their mortgage on their house each fortnight they set up an automatic payment (AP) for $416.30 to come out each and every fortnight. On the 6th of May the automatic payment goes into a loan account that they have with the same bank (notice the different suffix number of 05 which is their loan account) to pay their mortgage. This payment reduces their bank balance to $278.96.

Samantha also has a part time job working school hours with Handy Andy's Appliances and is paid fortnightly. On the 6th May Samantha gets paid $320.04 from Handy Andy's Appliances who direct credit the money into their account. This increases their bank account to $599.00.

On the 7th May Samantha transfers $92.00 into their sharing account and their savings account. The amount is different from last week because Samantha gets paid this week as well. This amount is 10% of $600.00 which is $60.00 and 10% of $320.00 which is $32.00 which makes $92.00. They also withdraw their cash money of $250.00 for the groceries, petrol and treats which reduces their bank balance to $165.00.

On the 13th May Simon gets paid $600.00 which increases their bank balance to $765.00.

On the 14th May Samantha goes into her local branch of Kiwi bank and asks them to transfer $60.00 into their sharing account (suffix 01) and their savings account (03) because they have been having trouble with their internet this week. This reduces their bank balance to $645.00.

On 17th May they withdraw $250.00. Ask your child can they remember what Simon and Samantha Silbo use this money for each week. (Food, petrol and treats). This reduces their bank account to $395.00.

On 20th May Simon gets paid $600.00 again which increases their bank balance to $995.00.

On the 20th May Samantha gets paid $320.04 which increases their bank balance to $1315.04.

On 20th May their mortgage of $416.30 is paid into their loan account which reduces their bank balance to $898.74.

On the 21st May they transfer $92.00 to their sharing account and $92.00 to their savings account and do their normal weekly withdrawal from the ATM of $250.00 which reduces their bank balance to $464.74.

On the 21st May Simon needs to go to the Medical Centre (doctor and chemist) a cost of $61.00 which reduces their bank balance to $403.74. He paid the bill using his Eftpos card.

On the 27th May Simon's wages of $600.00 are paid into their account which increases their bank balance to $1003.74.

On 28th May, Samantha by internet banking transfers $60.00 into their sharing account and $60.00 into their savings account. This reduces their bank balance to $883.74.

On 28th May at the ATM in Springfield they take out $250.00 cash for their shopping, petrol and treat money which reduces their bank balance to $633.74.

On 28th May Contact Energy take out $160.00 from their bank account by direct debit to pay for their power bill. This reduces their bank balance to $473.74.

On 31st May the bank takes out $5.00 as a fee for servicing their account which reduces their bank balance to $468.74.

The next part of the story would start as Simon and Samantha Silbo begin the month of June with an opening bank balance of $468.74.

So after one month of using the Triple S P System, Samantha and Simon have paid all their bills because they told their money where to go instead of wondering where it went.

They have also saved $364.00 this month. They have set a Smart Goal of saving $1000.00 which they would put into a term investment for the future.

They also have $364.00 in their account to share with others. They could sponsor a child from overseas, buy groceries, or support their favourite charity.

Use one of your old bank statements to go through and use it to "read a story" of what you have done with your own money over a week or month.

Note that different banks may use different abbreviations.

**"Learning by experience often is painful.
The more it hurts, the more you learn."**

Ralph Banks

Bank Statement for Simon and Samantha Silbo

KIWIBANK Level 11, 155 The Terrace Wellington		Account Name: Simon & Samantha Silbo
Transaction begin date	29 April 2008	Account number: 38 9010 9302204-02
Transaction end date	31 May 2008	

POSTED	DETAILS	DEBIT	CREDIT	BALANCE
29/04	OPENING BALANCE			246.48
29/04	ITEC Comp Services Ref: Simon wages		600.00	846.48
30/04	Bank fee	5.00		841.48
01/05	Transfer to S & S Silbo Sharing a/c 9302204-01	60.00		781.48
01/05	Transfer to S & S Silbo Saving a/c 9302204-03	60.00		721.48
01/05	POS 23443259648 Telecom mobile 12.45	10.00		711.48
01/05	ATM W/D Springfield 10.34	250.00		461.48
03/05	Direct Debit Slingshot	83.00		378.48
03/05	Bill Payment AMI Contents Insurance	283.22		95.26
06/05	ITEC Comp Services Ref: Simon wages		600.00	695.26
06/05	AP# 12387654 to S & S Silbo Loan repayment a/c 9302204-05	416.30		278.96
06/05	Handy Andys Appliances Ref: Sam. wages		320.04	599.00
07/05	Transfer to S & S Silbo Sharing a/c 9302204-01	92.00		507.00
07/08	ATM W/D Springfield 9.45	250.00		257.00
07/05	Transfer to S & S Silbo Saving a/c 9302204-03	92.00		165.00
13/05	ITEC Comp Services Ref: Simon wages		600.00	765.00
14/05	Transfer to S & S Silbo Sharing a/c 9302204-01	60.00		705.00
14/05	Transfer to S & S Silbo Saving a/c 9302204-03	60.00		645.00
17/05	ATM W/D Springfield 15.34	250.00		395.00
20/05	ITEC Comp Services Ref: Simon wages		600.00	995.00
20/05	Handy Andys Appliances Ref: Sam. wages		320.04	1315.04
20/05	AP# 12387654 to S & S Silbo Loan repayment a/c 9302204-05	416.30		898.74
21/05	Transfer to S & S Silbo Sharing a/c 9302204-01	92.00		806.74
21/05	Transfer to S & S Silbo Saving a/c 9302204-03	92.00		714.74
21/05	ATM W/D Springfield	250.00		464.74
21/05	POS 234 432 59649Central Medical Centre 8.30	61.00		403.74
27/05	ITEC Comp Services Ref: Simon wages		600.00	1003.74
28/05	Transfer to S & S Silbo Sharing a/c 302204-01	60.00		943.74
28/05	Transfer to S & S Silbo Saving a/c 302204-03	60.00		883.74
28/05	ATM W/D Springfield 10.55	250.00		633.74
28/05	Contact Energy Direct Debit	160.00		473.74
31/05	Bank Fee	5.00		468.74
	CLOSING BALANCE			468.74

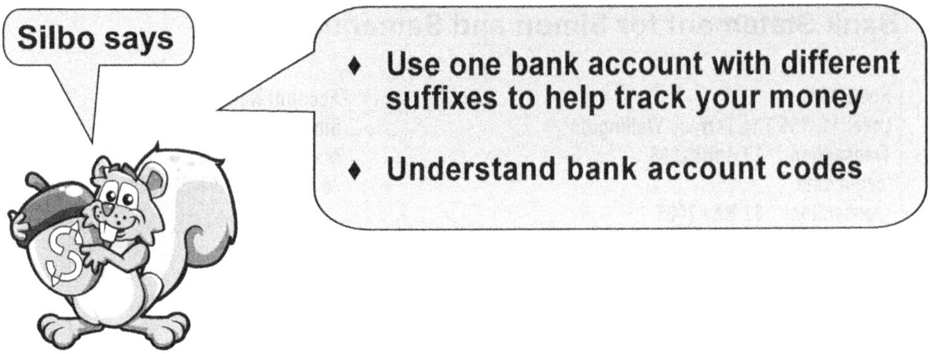

There is a principle that if you look after what you have got well then you may be entrusted with more in the future. Using different bank accounts for different purposes within the same bank can help manage your money more effectively. It is also important to understand what the numbers mean at the beginning of any bank account so that if you are asking people to pay money into your bank account that it does not get lost. It works the other way around as well. If you want to tell your money to go into someone else's account you don't want it to get lost either. We suggest you have three bank accounts (with the same labels as the money jars. One called Sharing, one called Savings and one called Spending. Each bank and branch in New Zealand and other banks around the world have their own code so money can be deposited into that account or arrangements can be made for regular expenses like your power account to be debited (taken directly from your account).

Sometimes through lack of knowledge people have large amounts of money sitting in a bank account earning as little as 1% interest. Using one bank account with different suffixes can help you transfer your money between different accounts to get your money working as hard as it can for you. If you don't look after your money now, then how can it look after you when you need it?

How to teach your child this important lesson

Go over the following activity and get your child to complete the exercise on filling out a deposit slip so they understand how the different numbers of a bank account work. Explain that the first six digits of bank codes in New Zealand serve as an identification code for each bank, branch and account number. So if someone's bank account number is 06 0413 123456 00, this 06 means that they have an account with the National Bank of New Zealand and the next four digits (0413) tells you that they have an account with the Rotorua branch of the National Bank of New Zealand. The next digits (1234567) are the actual account number and the final two digits (00) tell which type of account they have – such as an ordinary savings account or term deposit.

If you have internet banking, show your child how easy it is to transfer money between different accounts to get your money working harder.

Find out from a bank what different types of accounts you can have under the main account. Ask about minimum balances you need for higher interest rates. Also ask about fees to withdraw money.

Banks within New Zealand and around the world have different numbers that identify them uniquely, so when someone is making or withdrawing from a bank account, it comes out from the right account, at the right branch and right country.

This is an example of a few banks in New Zealand.

Bank Number	Name of Bank
01	ANZ Banking Group (NL) Limited
02	Bank of New Zealand Ltd
03	Westpac Banking Corporation
06	The National Bank of New Zealand Limited
38	Kiwibank

Smart Sam banks with Kiwi Bank at the branch in Ngongotaha and has three different types of bank accounts.

38 9005 2222876:00 Cheque account earning 0% interest

38 9005 2222876:01 Savings account earning 5% interest

38 9005 2222876:02 Term deposit account earning 7.65%% interest

If he had $5000.00 in the 00 account and didn't need it immediately, wouldn't it make sense to move it into the 01 account until he needed it? He could withdraw it anytime (check on any withdrawal fees) and still make good interest on it. If he knew he didn't need it for three months, he could put it into a term deposit which means that he is unable to withdraw it before a set date, or if he did, then he would lose some of the interest he had gained. Sometimes there could be exit fees as well.

How would you fill in a deposit slip to put money into Sam's savings account?

Kiwi bank Kiwibank Limited 155 The Terrace Wellington 	**DEPOSIT** Date_____/_____/_____	
Paid in by(signature)	Notes	
	Coins	
	Total cash	
Credit account of (please print)	Cheques	
	TOTAL	
38 9005 _ _ _ _ _ _ _ 0 _ _	(proceeds of cheques not available until cleared)	

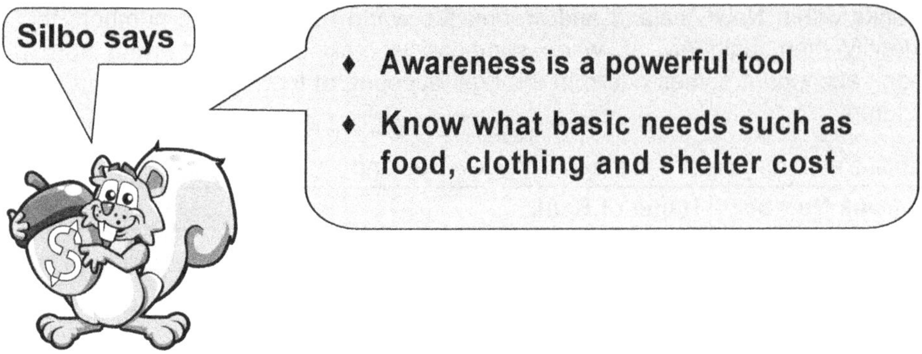

Most children don't really think about how much it costs to keep them. Your child may be surprised at how much money you as a parent spend on them. A word of caution – resist the temptation to keep saying things like – "Look how much you cost me". Explain that this is purely a learning experience for them to understand what certain things do cost and how much it actually cost to raise a family. Instil in your child that he or she is worth it – that you love them, and that having them was the best choice that you ever made!

Your child, or you for that matter may not have an accurate picture of what things actually cost because in the past many parents have not discussed what all the little things added up to. This activity can be a real eye opener for your child whether you are a family on an above, middle or below average income.

How to teach your child this important lesson

See if your child can guess how much it costs each week or year on various expenses and then give him the real figures. Work out a weekly amount and then multiply by 52 weeks to get a yearly amount. For example: Your food is $200.00 per week for five of you. Divide $200.00 by 5 = $40.00 x 52 weeks = $2080.00 per person per year.

This can be a great time to discuss "needs" and "wants". What things were really necessities? What things were bought from "pressure" from unseen forces such as advertising or peer pressure?

Let your child see how frustrating it can be for you when they constantly ask for "stuff" when the spending was not planned for.

What does it cost my family for me to live at home?

	Average per week	Average per year
Groceries: To feed me costs my family	$________	$________
Clothing: Maybe 3 set of clothes every year	$________	$________
Doctors visits: I only go to the Doctors once a year	$________	$________
Education: Books and trips and things for school	$________	$________
Power: My share of the power bill	$________	$________
Telephone & Internet: Because I use the internet	$________	$________
Haircuts: To keep looking cool, maybe 4 per year	$________	$________
New shoes: My last pair cost $________ x 2 per yr	$________	$________

ON A WEEKLY BASIS THAT WOULD BE $______________

OVER A YEAR THAT ADDS UP TO $______________

Plus there's all the other stuff like

Going on a family holiday somewhere special $________

Occasional movie treats or videos to keep us out of mischief! $________

Money for me to buy my lunch occasionally $________

When I need to buy a birthday present for someone $________

What else might my parents spend money on?

- **Most people don't plan to fail, they fail to plan**
- **A sharing and savings plan is a tool to help you reach your dreams**

A Sharing, Savings and Spending Plan is a tool to help you reach your dreams. It is a plan for you to tell your money where to go instead of wondering where it went. Another way of saying this is a "cash flow forecast" – which means you put on paper a record of telling your money where to go instead of wondering where it went. If you are one of the New Zealanders who are spending $1.14 for every dollar they earn (source NZ Department of Statistics) then this is the first step to taking charge. Start by collecting all the information you need.

If you don't know what expenses are coming up and planning for them accordingly, you can get into a position where your money is controlling you instead of the other way around. Many adults who are financially sick view a sharing, savings and spending plan (the triple S Plan) as something that limits or restricts them instead of a wonderful tool to help them now and to plan for their future.

How to teach your child this important lesson

As mentioned before, the first place to start completing a Sharing, Savings and Spending plan is to collect all the information you need to put in the Plan. You need to know what money is coming in, to the cent, and what is going out to the cent. Go through each item with your child and get him to help you fill in the information on each page.

Doing this exercise is a great way to collect all your financial information into one place. Then you will have one place where you can check how much things cost and when they are due. This can take quite a bit of time, however many people when they do this exercise find it worthwhile. They will find things such as they have been paying for contents insurance for their house with two insurance companies or they have paid a bill twice without realising it. It is also a great time, to think about what you want to spend your money on.

> **"Some people plan their holidays better than they plan their lives" Author unknown**

- To convert monthly amounts to weekly amounts take your monthly amount and multiply it by 12 and then divide it by 52.
- To convert fortnightly amounts to weekly amounts divide it by 2.
- To convert yearly amounts to weekly amounts divide by 52.
- To convert quarterly amounts to weekly amounts, multiply by four and divide by 52.

Before attempting to do a Sharing, Spending and Savings Plan (cash flow forecast) it is best to collect all your information first. Looking at your money week by week can make things a little clearer. Using the "Fact Finding Form", start to fill in the form below using the following steps.

Fill in "amount" which is what you actually pay.

Fill in "How often" (frequency paid) W= Weekly, FN=Fortnightly, M=Monthly, Q=Quarterly, 6M= 6 Monthly and finally A=Annually.

Fill in what dates these amounts are paid.

Then use the guide above to calculate the amounts into weekly amounts.

Listing all your outgoings may take some time. It is important to list everything. We suggest you fill out the form in pencil. The information has been grouped under different headings. At the end of each group add up the column. Write the total in the boxes at the bottom of each table.

You will find this a great tool when completed as you will know how much things cost, and when they are due.

***Note**: Sometimes amounts such as student loans, superannuation, and child support payments are taken out of your wages before you get them. It is best to take your actual pay you earn (minus tax) as your income and then put the student loan or what ever it is in the "expenses column", so you can actually see where your money goes.*

"Don't judge each day by the harvest you reap but by the seeds that you plant." <u>Robert Louis Stevenson</u>

FACT FINDING FORM

INCOMING

	Weekly $	Amount $	How often	When due
My wages/salary (after tax) but before other deductions				
My partners wages/salary (after tax) but before other deductions				
Benefits				
Student allowance				
Supplements				
Child maintenance				
Odd jobs				
Board or rent paid to me				
Interest or earnings from investments				
Income from business				
Other				
TOTAL:				

OUTGOING

SHARING WITH OTHERS	Weekly $	Amount $	How often	When due
World Vision				
Tear fund				
Church				
SPCA				
Other				
TOTAL:				

SAVINGS				
Term deposit				
House				
Retirement				
Holiday				
Education				
Incidentals				
Other				
TOTAL:				

ACCOMMODATION	Weekly $	Amount $	How often	When due
Rent				
Board				
TOTAL:				

FOOD				
Weekly/fortnightly supermarket shopping				
Takeaway food and drinks				
Bought school lunches				
Lunches out				
Dinners out				
Snacks				
Other				
TOTAL:				

UTILITIES				
Electricity				
Gas				
Telephone and Internet				
Mobile Phone				
Water				
Rates				
TOTAL:				

DEBTS				
Mortgage payments				
Car payments				
Hire purchase (1)				
Hire purchase (2)				
Personal loan				
Credit card (1)				
Credit card (2)				
Student loan				
Store card				
Unpaid bills that are behind eg phone, power.				
Other:				
TOTAL:				

TRANSPORT	**Weekly $**	**Amount $**	**How often**	**When due**
Vehicle licensing				
Warrant of Fitness				
Buses/trains/taxis				
Petrol/diesel				
Motor vehicle repairs				
TOTAL:				

EDUCATION				
School fees				
Continuing education courses				
Tertiary fees				
Books etc				
Other:				
TOTAL:				

MEDICAL				
Doctor				
Chemist prescriptions				
Chemist other				
On going medical expenses				
TOTAL:				

INSURANCE				
Home				
Contents				
Health				
Life				
Vehicle				
Other				
TOTAL:				

OTHER EXPENSES				
Bank fees				
Entertainment				
Holidays				
Clothes				
Sports/hobbies/clubs				

OTHER EXPENSES continued	Weekly $	Amount $	How often	When due
Alcohol				
Cigarettes				
Toiletries				
Gifts				
Child support payments/ other				
TOTAL:				

Take the total amount from each of the tables above and write the amounts beside the categories in the table below. Then add up the columns to find your weekly and monthly total outgoings.

COMBINED TOTALS	Weekly $	Amount $
Sharing total		
Savings total		
Accommodation total		
Food total		
Utilities total		
Debts total		
Transport		
Education total		
Medical total		
Insurance total		
Other expenses total		
TOTAL:		

Now write your Total Incomings and your Total Outgoings in the table below.

Then subtract your Total Outgoings from your Total Incomings to find out your financial situation.

MOMENT OF TRUTH	Weekly $	Amount $
Total incomings		
Total outgoings		
YOUR FINANCIAL SITUATION + -		

Don't panic if your outgoings are more than your incomings. In the next lesson we will look at trimming which will help you reduce some unnecessary expenses.

- **Use the Triple SP system to become and stay financially well**
- **Track in and out every cent of your money**

Many people have not been trained how to do a Sharing, Savings and Spending plan. Many people who have not planned where they allocate their money are very easily persuaded by sales people, to buy "stuff" that they don't really need.

Because people have not planned how they will allocate their money, they can quickly end up in debt because they buy things on a "whim". When you have a plan and you stick to it, it is so much easier to say to your children, when they ask for the latest toy or takeaway "Lets look at our Triple S P plan before we decide", or "Silbo says delay your decision to purchase for 24 hours" is better than feeling pressed into making a decision right then. From personal experience this works equally well with anyone who wants you to spend money that you have not planned for. Salespeople often haven't been trained to have an answer when you say to them "I'll need to consult my spending and savings plan first".

How to teach your child this important lesson

Go through the spending and savings plan on the following page. Simon and Samantha have done the "Fact Finding Form" and have collected all their financial information. They now are able to fill in the plan and be able to forecast how their cash-flow is going to look over the next 12 months. They are able to plan around their cash flow and know exactly how their financial situation should be at any given time. Each item is planned for carefully.

For the week commencing 29th April, Simon and Samantha "carried forward" some money from the previous week of $248.48. There was $600.00 income that week which made a total of $846.48 available to spend. The total planned spending (payments) for that week was $751.22 which when taken away from the total available funds of $846.48 leaving a balance of $95.26 to be carried forward to next week and so the process is repeated the next week and so on. Explain that even though sometimes there seems to be a surplus in the bank, that it is necessary to keep it there. Look at the week of 24th June and notice that $450.00 rates are paid and then the following week the mortgage of $416.30 is paid. If Samantha or Simon Silbo had just looked at their bank balance and spent what was left that week, then they would not have had been able to pay their rates one week and their mortgage the following week. Explain also that your bank statement should be used as a confirmation that your money has gone where you told it to go, not telling you where it went!

Sam and Simon Silbo payments as and when due

Date pay goes in	29 Apr	6 May	13 May	20 May	27 May	3 Jun	10 Jun	17 Jun	24 Jun	1 Jul	8 Jul	15 Jul
Carried forward	$246.48	$95.26	$165.00	$395.00	$403.74	$458.74	$445.48	$420.48	$490.22	$95.22	$81.96	$311.96
INCOME AMOUNTS												
Simon - wages	600.00	600.00	600.00	600.00	600.00	600.00	600.00	600.00	600.00	600.00	600.00	600.00
Samantha wages		320.04		320.04		320.04		320.04		320.04		320.04
Other												
TOTAL INCOME	600.00	920.04	600.00	920.04	600.00	920.04	600.00	920.04	600.00	920.04	600.00	920.04
Total Available	**846.48**	**1,015.30**	**765.00**	**1,315.04**	**1,003.74**	**1,378.78**	**1,045.48**	**1,340.52**	**1,090.22**	**1,015.26**	**681.95**	**1,232.00**
SPENDING												
Sharing into separate a/c	60.00	92.00	60.00	92.00	60.00	92.00	60.00	92.00	60.00	92.00	60.00	92.00
Saving into separate a/c	60.00	92.00	60.00	92.00	60.00	92.00	60.00	92.00	60.00	92.00	60.00	92.00
Food (cash)	150.00	150.00	150.00	150.00	150.00	150.00	150.00	150.00	150.00	150.00	150.00	150.00
Petrol (cash)	80.00	80.00	80.00	80.00	80.00	80.00	80.00	80.00	80.00	80.00	80.00	80.00
Treats	20.00	20.00	20.00	20.00	20.00	20.00	20.00	20.00	20.00	20.00	20.00	20.00
Periodic spending												
Mortgage		416.30		416.30		416.30		416.30		416.30		416.30
Power					160.00				160.00			
Telephone/broadband	83.00					83.00				83.00		
Cell phone	10.00				10.00				10.00			
Rates									450.00			
Car wof and licencing							55.00					
Car maintenance							200.00					
Education/school fees												
Doctor				55.00								
Chemist				6.00								
House insurance												
Contents insurance	283.22											
Life insurance												
Vehicle insurance												196.64
Gifts												
Clubs												
Sports												
Other												
Bank fees	5.00				5.00				5.00			
Student loan												
TOTAL PAYMENTS	**751.22**	**850.30**	**370.00**	**911.30**	**545.00**	**933.30**	**625.00**	**850.30**	**995.00**	**933.30**	**370.00**	**1,046.94**
C/F BALANCE	95.26	165.00	395.00	403.74	458.74	445.48	420.48	490.22	95.22	81.96	311.96	185.06

Silbo says

- **Looking at a cash-flow forecast weekly can help make things clearer**
- **For every action there is a reaction**

Many people go to the ATM (automatic teller machine) to see how much money they have in the bank and this is how they decide what they have to spend. If you are one of those people who don't accumulate the extra in your spending account for those items such as car licensing, car repairs/maintenance, life becomes more stressful than it should. There are many ways to do a "Triple S Plan". So in the following example we have done a plan where the money is allocated weekly instead of when it is actually paid so you get the idea that in theory "it is actually spent" even though the money is still showing in your bank account.

When you overspend money which is not planned for it has to come from another area of your finances. Because, for every action, there is a reaction. Have you ever had to cut down on the amount of food you bought in any one week because of overspending in other areas in another week?

How to teach your child this important lesson

Go through with your child the following "Triple S Plan" for the Silbo Family which uses the same figures as the previous example. However, this time the items are shown as being "spent" weekly. Explain why it is important to keep the money in your bank account so it can be "paid out" at the correct time. If you overspend in one area, then it will put stress on your finances in another area.

Share with your child times when you spent what you had in the bank only to discover you had a big bill to pay two weeks later and it made your life stressful unnecessarily and what consequences followed from that. Did you have to cut down on food? Did you have to borrow? Were you late paying a bill and so incurred a penalty? These are just some examples.

Saving and Spending plan showing money being allocated for expenses on a weekly basis

Date pay goes in	29 Apr	6 May	13 May	20 May	27 May	3 Jun	10 Jun	17 Jun	24 Jun	1 Jul	8 Jul	15 Jul
Carried forward	$246.48	118.40	246.36	118.28	246.24	118.16	246.12	118.04	246.00	117.92	245.88	117.80
INCOME AMOUNTS												
Simon - wages	600.00	600.00	600.00	600.00	600.00	600.00	600.00	600.00	600.00	600.00	600.00	600.00
Samantha wages		320.04		320.04		320.04		320.04		320.04		320.04
Other												
TOTAL INCOME	600.00	920.04	600.00	920.04	600.00	920.04	600.00	920.04	600.00	920.04	600.00	920.04
Total Available	**846.48**	**1,038.44**	**846.36**	**1,038.32**	**846.24**	**1,038.20**	**846.12**	**1,038.08**	**846.00**	**1,037.96**	**845.88**	**1,037.84**
SPENDING												
Sharing into separate a/c	60.00	92.00	60.00	92.00	60.00	92.00	60.00	92.00	60.00	92.00	60.00	92.00
Saving into separate a/c	60.00	92.00	60.00	92.00	60.00	92.00	60.00	92.00	60.00	92.00	60.00	92.00
Food (cash)	150.00	150.00	150.00	150.00	150.00	150.00	150.00	150.00	150.00	150.00	150.00	150.00
Petrol (cash)	80.00	80.00	80.00	80.00	80.00	80.00	80.00	80.00	80.00	80.00	80.00	80.00
Treats	20.00	20.00	20.00	20.00	20.00	20.00	20.00	20.00	20.00	20.00	20.00	20.00
Periodic spending												
Mortgage	208.15	208.15	208.15	208.15	208.15	208.15	208.15	208.15	208.15	208.15	208.15	208.15
Power	36.92	36.92	36.92	36.92	36.92	36.92	36.92	36.92	36.92	36.92	36.92	36.92
Telephone/broadband	19.15	19.15	19.15	19.15	19.15	19.15	19.15	19.15	19.15	19.15	19.15	19.15
Cell phone	2.30	2.30	2.30	2.30	2.30	2.30	2.30	2.30	2.30	2.30	2.30	2.30
Rates	34.16	34.16	34.16	34.16	34.16	34.16	34.16	34.16	34.16	34.16	34.16	34.16
Car wof and licencing	5.77	5.77	5.77	5.77	5.77	5.77	5.77	5.77	5.77	5.77	5.77	5.77
Car maintenance	7.69	7.69	7.69	7.69	7.69	7.69	7.69	7.69	7.69	7.69	7.69	7.69
Education/school fees	6.88	6.88	6.88	6.88	6.88	6.88	6.88	6.88	6.88	6.88	6.88	6.88
Doctor	4.23	4.23	4.23	4.23	4.23	4.23	4.23	4.23	4.23	4.23	4.23	4.23
Chemist	0.46	0.46	0.46	0.46	0.46	0.46	0.46	0.46	0.46	0.46	0.46	0.46
House insurance	8.47	8.47	8.47	8.47	8.47	8.47	8.47	8.47	8.47	8.47	8.47	8.47
Contents insurance	5.44	5.44	5.44	5.44	5.44	5.44	5.44	5.44	5.44	5.44	5.44	5.44
Life insurance												
Vehicle insurance	3.78	3.78	3.78	3.78	3.78	3.78	3.78	3.78	3.78	3.78	3.78	3.78
Gifts												
Clubs												
Sports												
Other	7.69	7.69	7.69	7.69	7.69	7.69	7.69	7.69	7.69	7.69	7.69	7.69
Bank fees	1.15	1.15	1.15	1.15	1.15	1.15	1.15	1.15	1.15	1.15	1.15	1.15
Student loan												
Surplus	5.84	5.84	5.84	5.84	5.84	5.84	5.84	5.84	5.84	5.84	5.84	5.84
TOTAL PAYMENTS	**728.08**	**792.08**	**728.08**	**792.08**	**728.08**	**792.08**	**728.08**	**792.08**	**728.08**	**792.08**	**728.08**	**792.08**
C/F BALANCE	118.40	246.36	118.28	246.24	118.16	246.12	118.04	246.00	117.92	245.88	117.80	245.76

NOTES

Step 6

"The poorest of all men is not the man without a cent but the man without a vision."

(Author unknown)

Silbo says

- **Dreaming about what you want in life is a good place to start with goal setting**
- **Close your eyes and dream about what could be, not what could have been**

Setting goals is one of the main ways people accomplish their dreams. Getting your child to learn the habit of setting goals (and dreaming, which they do naturally) is a great first step in helping them become successful in life.

Until we sit down and contemplate what we want from life, we will always tend to "drift along" and not achieve our full potential. Having a notice-board or place on the wall to write up your dreams and goals is a great way to have a visual reminder of what you aspire to be or have. Many an idea will come to us, and while they are often a good idea, unless they are grabbed hold of and implanted into our mind they will soon pass by and never become the dream that pushes us to higher achievement. The way we implant that dream into our mind is to write it down and put it in a place where we can see it every day.

How to teach your child this important lesson

Using the next page as prompts start your child off with a pen, piece of paper, crayons, magazine etc and then help him to dream of what he would like for his future. You could start off with dreaming about a special holiday, where he would love to live, what type of car he would like, what he is passionate about and then lead into what job or career he might like. Once your child has some dreams written down he could find pictures of what the dream is about and then pin them to his wall as a visual reminder.

Families tend not to do this exercise of getting together and dreaming about what they would like for their family situation. Try out this exercise of writing down dreams as a family. You may be surprised at what is hiding in the minds of other family members.

Start dreaming about what you would like for your future.

Write your dreams on a board or paper and pin them to your wall.

What am I passionate about?

Helping others?

Career?

Rich and Famous?

Hobbies?

House?

Sports?

Stuff?

Car?

Friends?

Learn to play an instrument

Travel?

If you don't dream it, you will never see it.

Silbo says

- **A short term goal is one you can achieve in under a year**
- **A long term goal is one which will take over a year to achieve**

Goals give purpose and direction to your life. Personal goals help you stay focused on outcomes you have chosen for yourself. Even when set-backs occur, as they inevitably will, goals help you to re-focus on the outcomes you desire. It is helpful to have short-term goals and long-term goals.

It has been shown that the biggest difference between those who reach their goals and those who don't, is that the achievers write their goals down and review them often whereas the others don't. It is not until you actually start writing goals down that you realise the power of the written goal. The power comes from the visual reminder of the goal which causes you to reflect on the motivation to achieve that goal.

How to teach your child this important lesson

Have your child look at the dream-board they have just made and consider if that dream is something that can be achieved in the short-term or in the long-term. If your child is to realise their dream, they have to consider such questions as "What might need to happen to make this dream a reality?" "What sort of obstacles will I face?" "Why is this dream important to me?" "When do I want to achieve my goal?" By clarifying those points you can then move on to the next section about SMART goals and ways to help make your child's dreams a reality.

It is important to plan and set goals and to review them regularly as your circumstances in life change.

An excellent book to read on goal-setting which is more aimed at adults is "How you can set and achieve your goals" by Des Moss. Have your child go through goal-setting in other areas of his life: school, sports, music, friends, health etc. Plan a family holiday using a Triple S P (refer back to Step 5) to estimate costs for travel, distance, activities, food etc.

A goal is when your dream becomes a target (something you are aiming for).

♦ **If you are setting goals, you may as well make them SMART goals**

S	**Specific**	What do you want to achieve?
M	**Measurable**	How will you know when you have achieved your goal?
A	**Achieve**	How?
R	**Realistic**	Is this goal achievable?
T	**Timely**	A date when you will have reached this goal

Many people do not achieve goals because they are not "SMART" goals. Another reason some people do not achieve their goals is when things happen that are out of their control (such as losing their job) they don't review that same goal and simply set it again with a new deadline.

You sometimes set off on a path to achieve a goal, but because it is not specific you don't really know what exactly you are wanting, or it isn't realistic. In order to help you achieve your goals you need to have a method to analyse the goal to see if it is worth aiming for in the first place. This is where the SMART goal tool is so useful.

How to teach your child this important lesson

Go through the list on the next page and choose which one is a "Smart" goal.

Answers to SMART goal questions

I am going to buy another car for a maximum of $1000.

I am going to have my new car by Christmas day this year.

I am going to save $1000.00 by setting up an automatic payment of $30.00 per week into a savings account and not touch it.

I have a part-time job that earns $100.00 per week so I can save $30.00 per week.

I will have the money saved by 1st December this year so I can look for a car for Christmas.

Look through each of these statements and select the correct statement to make a SMART goal. Write the answer in the spaces below:

DATE GOAL SET: 1st March 2008

Which goal is specific?

I am going to buy another car for a maximum of $1000.

I am going to save some money to buy a car.

Which goal is measurable?

I am going to have my new car sometime.

I am going to have my new car by Christmas day this year.

How are you going to achieve it and is it achievable?

I earn $100.00 per week so I am going to save $1000.00 by next week.

I am going to save $1000.00 by setting up an automatic payment of $30.00 per week into a savings account and not touch it.

Which goal is realistic?

I have a part-time job that earns $100.00 per week so I can save $30.00 per week.

I have a part-time job that earns $100.00 per week so I can save $110.00 per week.

Which goal is timely?

I will have $1000.00 saved by sometime this year.

I will have the money saved by 1st December this year so I can look for a car for Christmas.

WRITE YOUR ANSWERS.

S ____

M ____

A ____

R ____

T ____

Write down some other sample goals and test to see if they are "SMART" goals.

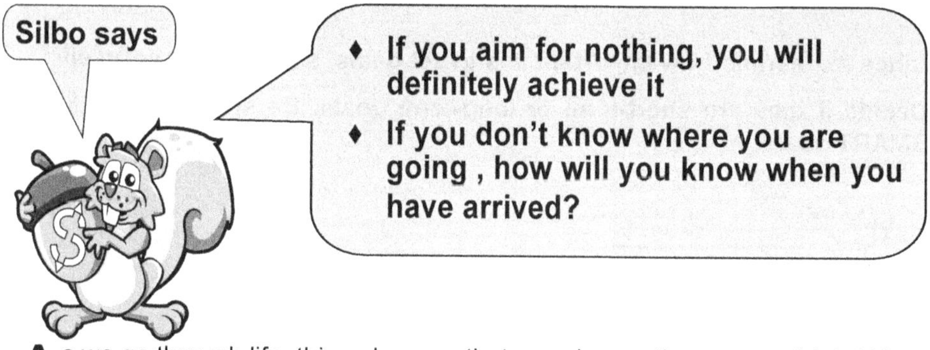

As we go through life, things happen that can change the way we think. When something happens that upsets your goal you need to review that goal and check that it still fits in with your life's purpose. It may mean that the goal is no longer valid, or it could just need an adjustment, such as the timing extended or shortened.

Goals give purpose and direction to your life. Personal goals help you to stay focused on outcomes you have chosen for yourself. Even when set-backs occur, as they inevitably will, goals help you to re-focus on the outcomes you desire. It is helpful to have short-term goals and long-term goals. The 'process' of reaching the goal is equally as important as actually reaching the goal. When a goal isn't reached – review it and re-set it again.

How to teach your child this important lesson

Ask your child to set some goals and to think about if they are short-term goals or long term goals. Your child could use one of the goals listed on his dream-board. Follow that with the three questions about the goal. Use the next page for this activity. Discuss how important it is to plan and set goals in order to accomplish the desired outcome. Put the date you set the goal on the page too.

"Success is not the result of spontaneous combustion. You must set yourself on fire." <u>Reggie Leach</u>

Since we learned how important it is to set goals, set some for yourself:

Decide if they are short-term or long-term goals. Be sure to make them SMART goals.

DATE____________________

My Goal is: ____

S ____

M ____

A ____

R ____

T ____

Why is this dream important? ____

____

What obstacles stand in the way? ____

____

What needs to happen to make this goal achievable?

____

____

Silbo says

- **If you want your needs in this life met, you must have faith and exercise it**
- **To achieve something it helps to visualise you have it already**

To start setting goals is foreign to many of us. Often we haven't been taught that it is an essential part of achievement. In order to achieve, we need to be able to see that the objective is possible. The way this happens is through visualising or imagining the end result.

Visualising that you already have what you set as a goal is part of the process in goal setting. The visualising tells you it is possible. If you can't imagine yourself as having achieved what you want, then you will be fighting an uphill battle to get to it. Call it positive thinking or the power of the mind, but these sayings highlight the effects of visualisation. "To think it about, is to bring it about", and "if you think you can, then you can, but if you think you can't, then you won't". In other words, you need to visualise the end result that you want to achieve in order for you to have something positive to aim for.

How to teach your child this important lesson

This next exercise is an opportunity for you and your child to start visualising the positive outcomes of dreams and goals. Take one of your child's goals and have him visualise it as a completed goal. As an example, take the example of the long-term goal of going to London in five years. Visualise saving for the holiday, means of transport, how long it took, any stopovers, interesting people you might meet and who met you at the other end etc.

Pretend you are writing a script for a story and filling in all the details of what it took to get to your child's goal. Explore all the possibilities to make this dream a visual reality by collecting pictures of possible events along the way.

> **"Too many people spend money they haven't earned, to buy things they don't want, to impress people they don't like."**
> **Will Rogers**

NOTES

Step 7

> **"I have enough money to last me the rest of my life, unless I buy something."**
>
> **<u>Jackie Mason US comedian (1934 - ?)</u>**

- **If you want your needs in this life met, you must have faith and exercise it**
- **To achieve something it helps to visualise you have it already**

Have you ever wondered why you were "talked" into going into debt for something that depreciates as soon as you buy it? You are being deceived by four main groups in society. These organisations have brainwashed you into thinking they are doing you favours, while in reality they're quietly and methodically picking your pockets and sucking the financial life out of you. Imagine them up in the Sky Tower in Auckland – looking over the whole country and saying – "The average New Zealander will earn between one and a half and three million dollars in their lifetime - how can we get most of it now while they are not thinking about the future?

Advertisers do a lot of psychological research into what makes you buy. It is their job to find ways that tap into your belief systems to get you to buy. Doctors are trained to look after your health. Accountants are trained to look after your finances. Advertisers are trained to use well thought-out marketing plans which change your belief systems over time. What you once thought was a "want", becomes a "need" and you buy unnecessarily even if it means sacrificing your long-term financial security.

Advertisers have created "emotional stories" that operate behind the scenes that affect your thinking and actions without you being consciously aware of what you are thinking about. Advertisements are designed so when you take on consumer debt (*items which depreciate as soon as they are bought, or personal loans to consolidate existing debt)*, they convey the feeling that you are sitting in a relaxing hot pool, which feels great. It's so peaceful and you won't have a care in the world. **Nothing could be further from the truth** because debt can cause you to worry, have health problems, cause relationship problems, and for some people commit crime. Consumer debt can cause you to become a modern day slave. A slave to your lender.

Consumer debt should be conveyed that when you take it on, all of a sudden you will realize you are in a swamp full of debt leeches who are sucking the financial life blood out of you and your family.

These leeches also seem to have the ability to crawl from one generation to another. After they have finished sucking the life blood from you they need to find new fresh blood – so they crawl and latch on to your children, and grandchildren. Unless you take action and kill those blood suckers once and for all, your short term gain will turn into a long term pain for you and your future generations.

Four main groups who deceive us are:

The *we need stuff* deceivers – (The Advertising Industry)

It is their job (how they get paid) to persuade us into believing that we need to drive the right kind of car, wear a particular brand of jeans, have no wrinkles and enjoy a holiday that you can't pay for fully now (just to name a few). They convince you that if you buy "stuff" it will make you happier, and appear that you are a more financially successful person (even if that affects the amount of food you can put on the table each week or you aren't able to pay all your bills fully). The truth is we need to learn to be happy with or without "stuff". The advertising industry has gradually changed our thinking so we believe that "wants" are actually "needs". Some people work harder or jeopardise their future retirement lifestyle by buying these imaginary "needs" when they are actually just "wants". Delayed gratification is something missing from our society – we have become a "I must have it now" society.

The *promoting* deceivers (The Media industry)

The media industry use their airwaves to promote 'social stories' that we must 'be' a certain way, 'look' a certain way or 'have' certain things to be happy. They can be very convincing telling us that we deserve things now when really we should be saving towards our future financial security.

The *supply* deceivers (The retailers)

Some retailers offer goods on sale that you 'must have' to be happier (even if you can't pay cash). How often have you seen advertisements that say 30% off today only and you go back the next day or next week and the sign says the same thing?

The *solution* deceivers (The lending industry)

The credit industry steps in when you really want to buy that lounge suite that will just look lovely and make you feel prosperous. They convince you can afford it because of low weekly payments (even though you haven't been able to save enough to buy it in the first place!). They make themselves out to be the rescuer – the answer to all your problems. They will say "We are here to help you and charge a little thing called interest for our help". When you have stretched yourself to the limit, they step in again and want to "help" you further. The reality is they charge you a higher rate of interest and put you even further into bondage as a slave to your lender.

How to teach your child this important lesson

Look at the way the world tries to convince us we need to do what other people want us to do (remember the exercise we did in step 2 when we looked at the emotions that are used to get us to buy things).

The *we need things* deceivers	The Advertising Industry
The *promoting* deceivers	The Media industry
The *supply* deceivers	The Retailers
The *solution* deceivers	The Lending industry

Now look at these statements and see if you can recognise which category they might belong to.

But wait! If you buy in the next 15 minutes, you will receive this set of steak knives absolutely free.

SALE,
TODAY
ONLY!!

To be cool, you need these latest designer jeans.

To have perfect skin, you need this product.

ONLY AVAILABLE FROM THE BEST STORES IN TOWN!!

Consolidate your debts with us. We have the best interest rates in town.

- **Increasing your income isn't always the answer**
- **You can't change your past but you can design your future**
- **Trim your debt by using a debt elimination plan**

Many adults think that "if I only had more income, I wouldn't struggle with my finances". The truth is that you need to control your spending by looking into everything you spend on a regular basis. The "Tracking" part of the system is about looking at what has happened in the past (and as much as you might want to change it – you can't!). The "Target" part of the system is looking to the future, putting your money to work for you for the future. The "Trimming" part of the system – is the present – what you have today, trimming out any unnecessary expenses and especially getting rid of debt!

Because many parents think that earning more is the only answer, (and not trimming what they are spending) they don't take the time to analyse their spending. They just work harder and harder, take on loans which they think will help, but all it does is put them further into financial bondage as they become a slave to their lender.

How to teach your child this important lesson

Talk your child through the following case study to see how an accelerated debt elimination plan works. A cousin of the Silbo family, Cynthia, has got herself into debt and has now decided to use an accelerated debt elimination plan to get out of debt as fast as possible. She has decided to trim her expenses by not buying two take away coffees each week (save $7.00) and reduce her food bill by $3.00 which means she can dedicate an extra $10.00 per week to pay off her debt. This $10.00 is called a debt accelerator amount. Look at the time difference just $10.00 per week makes. She will be debt free ten months earlier. Once she is debt free she could save that same $124.00 per week that was being used to pay off debt and after a year she would have saved $7448.00 and after two years she would have saved $14,896.00.

A debt elimination plan works likes this. Start with paying off the smallest debt first (or the one with the least payments still owing). This will give you a sense of achievement. You find out what your normal repayment is and then you add your debt acceleration amount to it. When that debt is paid off you add what you were paying already to the next debt and this is where the acceleration part starts. Many people when finishing off paying one debt just spend the extra, however if you realised that you won't have any less money to spend (as the money was already committed to paying off debt) you could be debt free much sooner. If you have consumer debt then make a list of each debt using the case study as a guide and decide today that you are going to work towards paying off your debt and make a pledge to not take on dumb debt.

Decide on a **debt acceleration amount.**

Step One Start with the smallest amount left or the least payments left

Step Two Write down each debt and name it

Step Three Write down the outstanding balance

Step Four Write down the regular weekly/monthly payment

Step Five Then add the accelerator amount to the first payment

Step Six When that debt is paid off add what you were paying in payments to the next debt payments and so on until you are finished.

Before starting the debt elimination plan Cynthia's car would be paid off on 24.07.2008, her dryer on 24.05.2012, her table on 03.09.2012 and her credit card on 03.12.2009.

Start with the smallest debt or the one with the least number of payments left.

Interest has not been included for the credit card so the actual time would be longer.

	Debt 1		Debt 2		Debt 3		Debt 4	
	Car loan		Dryer		Table		Credit card	
Date	Amount	Balance	Amount	Balance	Amount	Balance	Amount	Balance
		889.50		425.00		458.00		3,360.00
01/05/08	**70.00**	**819.50**	2.00	423.00	2.00	456.00	40.00	3,320.00
08/05/08	80.00	739.50	2.00	421.00	2.00	454.00	40.00	3,280.00
15/05/08	80.00	659.50	2.00	419.00	2.00	452.00	40.00	3,240.00
22/05/08	80.00	579.50	2.00	417.00	2.00	450.00	40.00	3,200.00
29/05/08	80.00	499.50	2.00	415.00	2.00	448.00	40.00	3,160.00
05/06/08	80.00	419.50	2.00	413.00	2.00	446.00	40.00	3,120.00
12/06/08	80.00	339.50	2.00	411.00	2.00	444.00	40.00	3,080.00
19/06/08	80.00	259.50	2.00	409.00	2.00	442.00	40.00	3,040.00
26/06/08	80.00	179.50	2.00	407.00	2.00	440.00	40.00	3,000.00
03/07/08	80.00	99.50	2.00	405.00	2.00	438.00	40.00	2,960.00
10/07/08	80.00	19.50	2.00	403.00	2.00	436.00	40.00	2,920.00
17/07/08	19.50	-	**62.50**	**340.50**	2.00	434.00	40.00	2,880.00
24/07/08			82.00	258.50	2.00	432.00	40.00	2,840.00
31/07/08			82.00	176.50	2.00	430.00	40.00	2.800.00
07/08/08			82.00	94.50	2.00	428.00	40.00	2,760.00
14/08/08			82.00	12.50	2.00	426.00	40.00	2,720.00
21/08/08			12.50	-	**71.50**	**354.50**	40.00	2,680.00
28/08/08					84.00	270.50	40.00	2,640.00
04/09/08					84.00	186.50	40.00	2,600.00
11/09/08					84.00	102.50	40.00	2,560.00
18/09/08					84.00	18.50	40.00	2,520.00
25/09/08					18.50		**105.50**	**2,414.50**
02/10/08							124.00	2,290.50
09/10/08							124.00	2,166.50
16/10/08							124.00	2,042.50
23/10/08							124.00	1,918.50
30/10/08							124.00	1,794.50
06/11/08							124.00	1,670.50
13/11/08							124.00	1,546.50
20/11/08							124.00	1,422.50
27/11/08							124.00	1,298.50
04/12/08							124.00	1,174.50
11/12/08							124.00	1,050.50
18/12/08							124.00	926.50
25/12/08							124.00	802.50
01/01/09							124.00	678.50
08/01/09							124.00	554.50
15/01/09							124.00	430.50
22/01/09							124.00	306.50
29/01/09							124.00	182.50
05/02/09							124.00	58.50
12/02/09							**58.50**	-

Cynthia starts her debt elimination plan by paying an extra $10.00 per week off the repayments. On 17.07.08 the car is paid off so she puts the balance of that payment towards the dryer. On the 24.07.08 she adds the whole amount of car money ($80.00) towards the dryer so now has $82.00 per week being paid off the debt. On 21.08.08 the dryer is paid off so she puts the balance of that payment towards the table debt. On the 28.08.08 she adds the whole amount of dryer payment plus the car money towards the table debt. On the 25.09.08 the table is paid off so she puts the balance of that payment towards the credit card debt. On the 02.10.08 she puts the whole amount from the dryer, table and the car towards the credit card debt. She is now paying $124.00 per week off the credit card debt which results in it being paid off 10 months early and her being debt free.

Step Seven

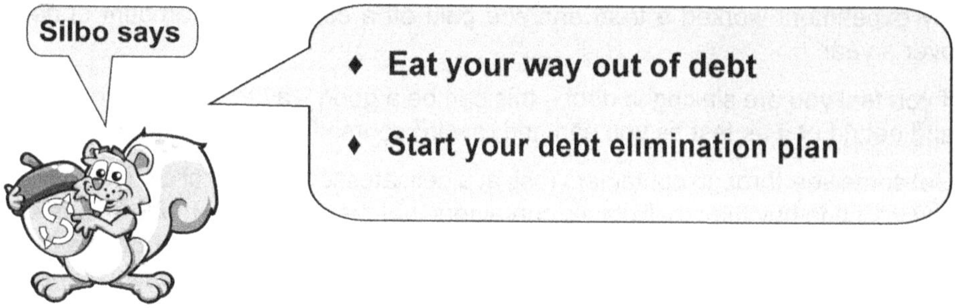

Many people cannot grasp how much debt they have in a tangible way. That is because they just look at figures on a piece of paper so it is not real to them. They can become sidetracked so easily from getting rid of debt.

This makes it hard for them to keep focusing on getting rid of their debt because they can't see it and experience the reality of it going down. By using a visual representation of what you owe you can become more focused on getting rid of debt.

How to teach your child this important lesson

Here is a fun way to start a debt elimination plan. My friend was finding it difficult to see how much debt she had in a tangible way. It was just figures on a piece of paper to her. The many debts she had were holding her back in many areas of her life.

I had this idea "eat your way out of debt" so thought I would use her as an experiment to see if it would work. I bought her some clear plastic containers from the delicatessen counter at the supermarket for around 30 cents each and a big bag of Smarties which I knew she loved. I got her to label each container with the name of each debt such as "washing machine repairs" together with the amount owing and how much the regular payment amount was. The first debt she wanted to pay off was for the repairs she had done to her washing machine. That debt was $160.00. Her weekly payment was $10.00 per week, so each smartie was worth $10.00. So $160.00 divided by $10.00 = 16 smarties, so she put 16 smarties into the plastic container for that debt and so on for all her remaining debts. It made her see that it would take 16 weeks to pay off her debt of $160.00 at $10.00 per week. Nearly a third of a year! The first time she made a payment she rewarded herself by eating one smartie. She decided to trim her grocery bill by $10.00 every week. She then added $10.00 to her payment (this is called a debt acceleration amount) and started paying $20.00 per week off her washing machine repairs instead of $10.00 per week. Now she was able to eat 2 smarties each week and reduce the time it took to pay off that debt by eight weeks.

She started to see progress so instead of spending the extra $20.00 per week she now had she paid that towards her next debt which she was also paying off at $10.00 per week. So now she was paying off that debt at $30.00 per week and she started eating three smarties a week from that container. Soon that debt was gone too so she added the $30.00 a week she had been paying to the next debt so she was paying off $40.00 per week, so she could eat 4 smarties each week. By involving her children in the process they encouraged her as they wanted to help her "eat her debt" each week.

My experiment worked a treat and she paid off a considerable amount of debt over a year.

If you feel you are sinking in debt – this can be a good way to visualize your debt and get rid of it as fast as you can and reward yourself at the same time.

Get some see-through containers (ask at a delicatessen counter at a supermarket how much to buy the small plastic containers that they put ready-made salads etc in) and represent each debt with a lolly as a dollar amount of each payment as this will help you visualise what you owe. Each time you make a payment, take one lolly and eat it which rewards you for paying off debt. This also helps you see the debt slowly disappearing. If you use the debt acceleration elimination plan, then when you make extra payments, you get to eat extra lollies. It doesn't have to be a lolly, it can be anything that you like to eat.

Look at your debt accelerator plan and label each jar with one of the debts.

Go to the supermarket and buy enough chocolate smarties or similar so that you can put into the jar enough smarties to equal the debt.

For Example: If the debt is $540.00 and your weekly repayments are $10.00, then you can say each smartie is worth $10.00. So $540.00 divided by $10.00 = 54 smarties. Put 54 smarties into the jar. Every week or whenever you make a payment of $10.00, you can reward yourself by eating one smartie. If you increase your payment to $20 per week then you can have two smarties or the equivalent of the payment made. This way you can literally eat your way out of debt and feel good about having a treat at the same time.

Example:

Debt: $540.00

Weekly payment: $10.00

Each smartie is worth: $10.00

Number of smarties into jar: 54

Your turn:

Debt: $________

Weekly payment: $________

Each smartie is worth: $________

Number of smarties into jar:_____

Silbo says

- **A want and a need are very different**
- **Financial health is more important than social status**

Talking about our purchases as wants and needs helps us to determine how badly we have to have that item. If you must have something in order to survive, then you would class that as a "need" (eg. food). However if you must have something simply because all the neighbours have got one, then it is a "want "(eg Sky TV). Most wants are based on an emotional viewpoint whereas most needs come from a survival point. There is nothing wrong with buying some wants. Problems occur when our spending money on "wants" causes over spending which in turn causes us not to be able to pay things such as the power bill, which would be classified in the "need" category.

To evaluate the importance of a buying decision, you need to be able to tell if what you are about to spend your money on is a "need" or "want". This part of the decision-making process can save you from spending money on things that really are just satisfying an emotional gap and perhaps your money would be better spent elsewhere.

In our "money lessons for life" classes, we will often have big discussions on this topic. As an extreme example we might ask the question, is a fridge a want or a need? The thing to remember is if things were really bad financially ask yourself "could I live without it?" Most times the reality is we probably would survive. In the case of the fridge there's no doubt life could be a lot easier with it but we wouldn't die without it. My parents did not have a fridge for the first year they were married and they survived.

How to teach your child this important lesson

With your child, look at all the different items listed on your child's page and have your child determine if they are a "need" or a "want" Have him think about some of the things around your home (such as the dishwasher, toaster, lawnmower or microwave) and consider if they are needs or wants and could they manage without them?

Some of the items that appear as "wants" may in fact be planned for, which is great – so point that out. The lesson we want your child to learn here is the difference between "needs" and "wants". It is the purchasing of the "wants" without due thought and planning that can cause financial difficulty.

An item you "need" is something that is essential to you being able to survive.

An item you "want" is something that you could live without if you had to.

Which of these items is a "need" and which is a "want"?

Put a circle around the needs and a square around the wants

Think of some other "wants" and "needs" around your home.

Silbo says

- **Each and every dollar has the power to grow into a mighty money tree**
- **Each and every dollar wasted has lost the power to grow**

The following quote from an article by Mark Hansen and Robert Allen (The One Minute Millionaire) explains how important it is to look after each and every dollar. “You see, prosperous people don’t think a dollar “is just a dollar”. They imagine it is a seed, a money seed that has the power to grow into a huge money tree, giving off fruit to fulfil every one of their dreams. Every dollar is a money seed. Just like a tiny acorn contains the power to grow into a mighty oak tree, if you destroy an acorn, the oak tree inside also dies. So too, with a money seed”.

It is hard for children to imagine the benefit of putting aside a little amount each and every week from an early age. It is even harder for them to see the value in not spending their money on unnecessary “stuff” and putting it towards their savings instead. Once children understand the concept of how a little can turn into a lot with the help of compound interest, they can more readily accept the need for restraint with their spending. We look closer at compound interest in step eight, but this exercise introduces the idea of not spending on unnecessary “stuff” and saving the money instead.

How to teach your child this important lesson

Have your child think about how much they spent on “stuff” during the week or month. Now have him imagine if he was to save it every week for the next 50 years. Take the example of $2.00 per week for the next 50 years and look at how that is transformed with the power of compound interest of 7% per annum added daily. That would change from being $5,200 ($2 x 52 weeks x 50 years) and turn into $47,734.

Now look at $10.00 per week. Instead of being $26,000 ($10 x 52 weeks x 50 years) it would become $238,678.

We used a calculator found at
http://www.dinkytown.net/java/CompoundSavings.html

Sorted.org.nz has some great calculators on their web-site where you can work out savings from a lump sum and how your bank balance could grow with regular savings etc. Show your child your own investment calculations in a spread-sheet if you have them or show them several investment statements so they see how the money has grown over time.

Here's a little exercise for you. Use a calculator and work out the compound interest on the following. This website calculator will help. Different calculators give a slightly different result.

http://www.dinkytown.net/java/CompoundSavings.html

If every week for the next 30 years, you take $20.00 and put it into the bank at 7% interest, how much do you think you would have in the bank at that end of that time?

The answer is one of the numbers below.

$35,609.98 $162,496.00

$128,753.99 $85,310.58

$106,526.00 $55,845.81

Write your answer here ________________________________

Now what if you were to take $100.00 every week and do the same for the next 30 years. How much would you have then?

$226,783.00 $532,630.00

$453,818.67 $43,818.67

$764,881.00 $123,355.68

Write your answer here________________________________

THAT IS A LOT OF MONEY!!!

Taxation has not been taken into account – so it would be a lot less than that – it is just an example of what a small amount can grow into over a long time.

answers $106,526.00 $532,630

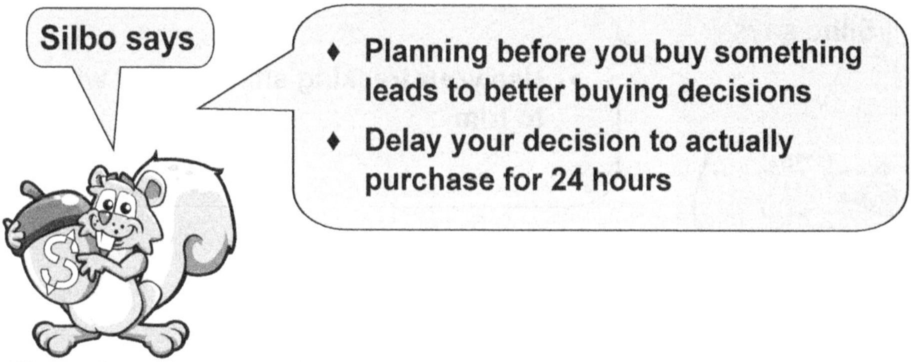

Spending money on whimsical "stuff" (stuff that goes down in value or has no value at all after you buy it), wastes an enormous amount of money that could be invested (put to work to grow) so you can be and stay financially well instead of being financially sick. Learning to be a wise consumer or smart shopper will help your child evaluate his purchasing decisions and hopefully waste less of his valuable money seeds.

Right from birth we get a subtle message to buy at all costs. In New Zealand people are now spending $1.14 for every dollar they earn by using credit. Common sense says this cannot continue. By continually buying things that are of no further use shortly after you buy them, you are putting your future retirement lifestyle in jeopardy.

How to teach your child this important lesson

Talk to your child about being beware of advertisements saying "buy two pairs and get one free" as retailers just want you to spend more of your hard earned cash. Think about the following scenario. You need one tee shirt and you have it in your mind that it should cost around $10.00. You go to the shop and see an advert that says "buy two T shirts for $25.00 and get one free". Many people then divide the cost by three which equals $8.33 each. You can think WOW – that's a good deal. However in reality, what has happened was that you went out planning to spend $10.00 but you spent $25.00. You spent $15.00 more than you intended to.

Let your child help you evaluate your next purchase. We suggest you make it a purchase you want for yourself, not something that they have an interest in as I don't think they will give you an unbiased view!

> Just five words spell prosperity, success and happiness.
>
> **"SPEND LESS THAN YOU EARN"**

You have seen how tracking can provide the key to what has been happening with your money in the past. You can now find areas where you can start to trim your expenses. Then you can put that money you trim by either paying off debt, if you have any, or putting it towards a short or long-term financial savings goal. Sometimes where you can trim expenses can be quite obvious – such as you buy a particular magazine per week for around $3.80 and one take-away coffee for around $4.00. Just cutting out these two can save $7.80 per week or $405.60 per year or $4,056 over ten years. Sometimes you have to delve a little deeper to find an amount to start the debt accelerator elimination process. Remember that you can't change the past, but you can design your future financial situation. Yesterday is history, tomorrow is a mystery, today is a gift, that is why we call it the present.

Sometimes people think they are doing a wise thing by starting saving when they still have debt. However it doesn't make good financial sense to be paying 19% interest on an outstanding balance on your credit card when you may only be receiving 8% on your money in an investment account. Learn to look at trimming expenses not as a sacrifice, but as a payment to yourself to help you achieve your most desired financial goals.

How to teach your child this important lesson

Go through your records where you have tracked how you have spent your money and discuss with your child ways in which you could reduce your spending. Look at each and every bill and look at where you could reduce spending. Look for times where you have had to pay extra fees such as using another bank's automatic teller machine, or missed the due dates on bills or had overdraft fees and therefore you had to pay extra. By paying your power bill just one day late could mean you lose a prompt payment discount of around $35.00.

Use the following headings over the page as a guide to see where you could reduce spending. Go through your bank statements for three months. Circle each amount that in hindsight you could have used to repay debt or saved. Look carefully at each amount under $10.00. Work through the example of paying your power bill one day late for ten years using losing a prompt payment discount of $35.00. *Answer $35.00 x 12 months = $420.00 per year or $4,200 over ten years.*

Have a look at the following and see if they are part of your life now or do you need to Trim them out or put them into your routine.

- Credit card Interest
- Unnecessary bank fees and extra charges
- Sky TV
- Power and phone and internet deals
- Early payment discounts
- Do you really need that second car?
- Late payment penalties
- Online instead of paper bank statements
- Grow your own vegetables
- Do you need to have call minder?
- Avoid unnecessary car travel
- Missed credit card payment penalties

What can you Trim?	How much would you save?	Extend your savings out over one year	Extend your savings out over ten years
Power late payment	$35.00	$420.00	$4,200.00
	$		
	$		
	$		
	$		

Use a calculator to work out how much your trimming would be worth if you were to invest it at 10% for 10 or 20 years.

Silbo Tip

Do a MENU for your week's meals.

Go shopping just ONCE a week or less often.

Have a SHOPPING LIST and STICK to it.

"The safest way to double your money is to fold it in half and sit on it."
(Kin Hubbard-1868-1930)

NOTES

Step 8

"Train a child in the way he should go, and when he is old he will not turn from it." <u>Proverbs 22:6</u>

- **Money makes the world go round**
- **Money that circulates, keeps the economy alive**

There is enough money to go round for everyone but to get it you have to think you can, then find a way to become a part of the money cycle.

Money goes round and round in a cycle. It gets handed from one person to the next and the same dollar note gets used until it becomes old and tattered. The money system allows for this torn and tattered note to be replaced with a new one and so the cycle continues again. By understanding the way money circulates, your child will be able to comprehend that with the right attitude and knowledge they can become part of the cycle and that there is no limit to the amount that they can access.

How to teach your child this important lesson

This is best done with a number of people, each playing a part in the use of a dollar. Stand in a circle with one person starting with a dollar. Have that person describe something they'd spend their money on, then work around the group as the money gets passed on and used with the next person in line describing what they do with it and how they pass it on. For example, I am a farmer and I need plants for my market garden, so I buy plants from the plant nursery. When my plants are ready I sell them to the market. The market then sells them to the restaurant. The market gardener decides to go to the restaurant for dinner. The restaurant uses up all its vegetables and has to go back to the market for more. The market then has to buy more vegetables from the farmer. The farmer then runs out of plants so he has to go back to the plant nursery, and so it goes on and on. Otherwise, simply go over the page by reading around the circle to see how money circulates.

The speed our economy grows or slows is determined by how we spend or hold on to what we earn. The faster we spend, the more money there is circulating and so the economy speeds up. If we hold on to our money, it doesn't circulate as fast so the economy slows down.

The money go round

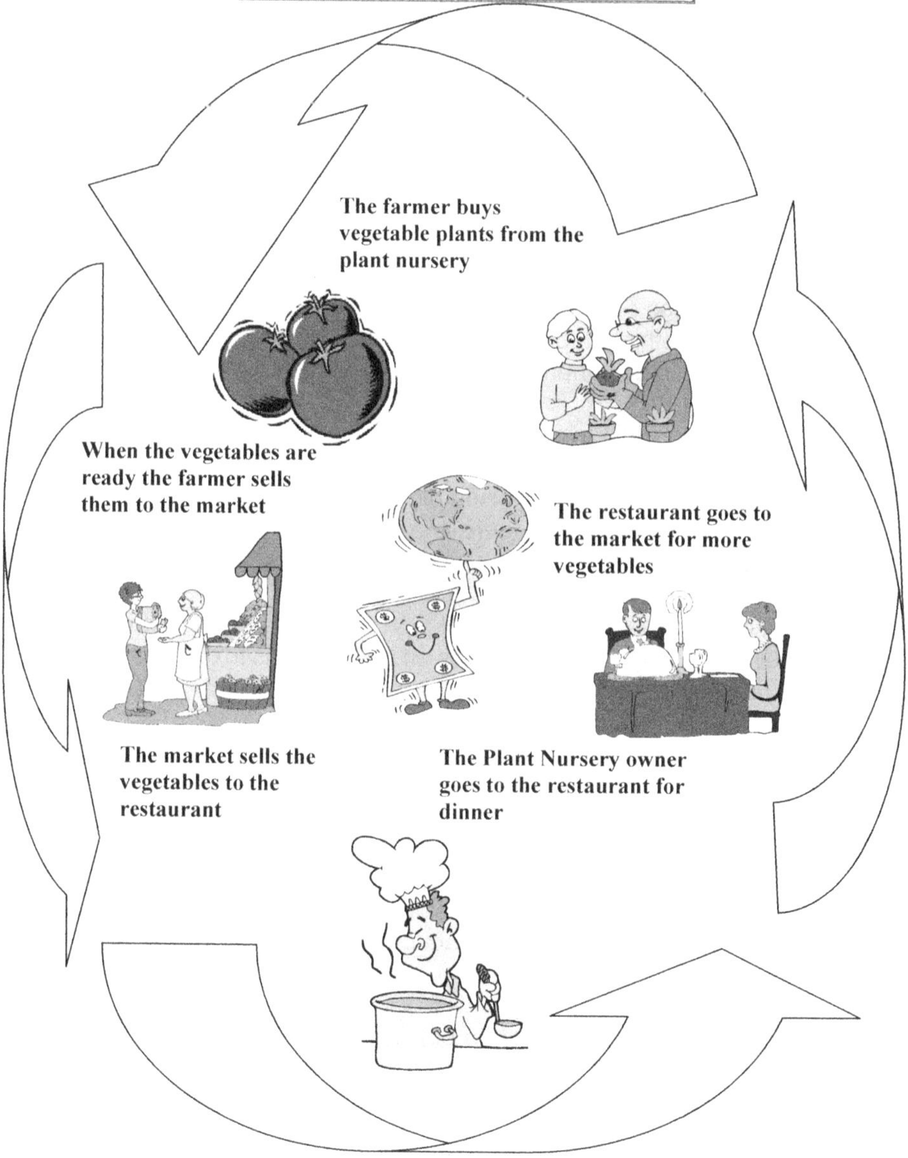

In times of economic uncertainty people, generally think twice before spending. This can lead to some businesses having to close or lay off staff. With the reduced spending, there is less money circulating and so the speed of the economy slows. As things improve and business gets better, unemployment gets better and so the ability to spend becomes easier thus resulting in the economy speeding up.

- **Supply and demand of goods and services affects the price we pay for things**
- **Bulk buying can give advantages and savings**

When people are talking about supply and demand, they are referring to when there is a shortage of something, the price often goes up and when there is an abundance of something, then the price will often go down. At the same time, if you are able to buy in bulk then you are able to negotiate a much better price.

It is important for your child to understand how supply and demand affects our everyday lives. When they see that petrol has gone up again, they sometimes think that the petrol station is just making big profits. What they don't see is that the oil producers overseas realise there is a shortage of oil and the demand is high so they can put the price up. The petrol companies have to then pass on the higher prices to the petrol stations that then pass the increase on to their customers. Likewise, when a supermarket buys a large quantity of an item, they are able to get it for cheaper and then pass on their savings to the customer. The better the buying power, then the better the savings.

How to teach your child this important lesson

Simply go through the next page with your child and look at how the price of oil affects things.

Talk about the fruit growing industry and use tomatoes as an example. Show how good and bad seasons can have an impact on the price people pay for fruit and vegetables.

When we owned our little grocery shop our customers would often complain at how much higher our prices were than at the supermarket. They thought we were making an amazing profit from them.

What they didn't realize was that because our buying power was very small we were not able to buy things at the same price as the big supermarkets (the effects of supply and demand).

Many times we would go to our wholesaler and buy a 500g of butter for $2.50 only to find that the nearest supermarket was selling the same butter for $2.20 (30 cents cheaper than we could buy it in the first place).

Production of oil goes down

Supply becomes less:

- Price of petrol goes up

which means:

- Transport costs go up
- Manufacturing cost goes up
- Cost of goods made from petroleum goes up (eg plastic)
- Cost to consumer goes up

Production of oil goes up

Supply becomes more:

- Price of petrol goes down

which means:

- Transport cost goes down
- Manufacturing cost goes down
- Cost to consumer goes down

A very good growing season for tomatoes

- Means there is a lot of tomatoes for sale in the shops - (an oversupply)
- Therefore prices go down otherwise the shop will be stuck with a lot of rotten tomatoes
- So the customer pays less

A bad growing season for tomatoes –

- means less tomatoes available
- Which then creates DEMAND
- This means the price of tomatoes goes up

SUPPLY vs DEMAND

Fill in the missing letters

When there is more supply of something than demand, then the price will go

D__________

When there is more demand for something than supply, then the price will go

U ____

- **There are lots of different costs that go into making something**
- **It is a myth that just because something costs more it must be better quality**

Brand alone does not mean that one product is any better than another. Often we find two identical products but with a huge price difference between them because one is a "brand" product and the other is not a "brand" product even though they may be made in the same factory.

To make the decision to purchase something, it helps to understand the steps a product goes through before it reaches the end customer. Once you can see that often there is no difference between a label product and a non label product and that they have just taken a different path to get to the shop, then it becomes easier to choose between the two.

You can buy a pair of "no name" jeans for example at $15.00 or a pair of "label jeans" at $100.00. It may be that the $100.00 jean material is slightly better quality but generally what makes up the huge difference is the costs that are added along the supply chain. These costs include huge advertising bills, lawyer's fees for branding and trade marking etc which have nothing to do with the quality of the goods. Many people "perceive it is better because of the name". "Label" milk is another example of where advertising, branding etc is paid for by the end consumer. The milk still comes out of a cow!

How to teach your child this important lesson

Look at the example of the cost of milk and talk with your child about the types of costs associated with producing it and how they all contribute to working out what the consumer will finally pay.

As something extra to do you could go to a wholesaler and look at their prices then go to a retail shop and compare prices. Talk about what makes the difference. Alternatively you could get your child to look on the internet at wholesale prices of something and then find a retail site to compare against.

THINK ABOUT THE COST OF MILK

It costs the same to get the milk from the cow but the different brands charge different prices - WHY IS THAT?

Companies charge different amounts for the same item because they often spend more on different parts of their business to get the product to you.

THINGS LIKE:

FREIGHT

TV ADVERTISING

LABOUR

FACTORY BUILDINGS

AND OTHER THINGS LIKE:

Advertising, insurance, repairs, rent, wages, sales representatives, research and development, administration and packaging,

All these things added together make up the price of something

Two companies make and sell the same item. Company "A" pays less rent than company "B". Which company could sell their product cheaper?

A or B

Answer: Company "A" doesn't pay as much for rent so will have more flexibility in what they charge for their product.

- **Banks and finance companies use your money to make their money**
- **Learn the difference between high and low risk investments**

When you put your money into a bank savings, term deposit, on line call account etc, you are lending your money to the bank. The bank (or finance company) then pays you interest to use your money to loan out to people and businesses. The bank or finance company charges the borrower more interest than it's paying you. That is how banks and finance companies make their money.

Certain types of investments carry higher potential risk but also bring higher potential reward. The other side of this is that investments that have a lower risk generally will receive a lower return on your money. It's important to understand this. Before you leap into any investment decision, there are some important rules you should follow: (refer to www.sorted.org.nz) for an expanded version of this).

1. Set your goals.
2. Know your risk profile.
3. Know how you want to invest your money.
4. Do your homework.
5. Research different companies' investment options.
6. Research the companies themselves.
7. Seek independent advice.
8. Spread your risk.

How to teach your child this important lesson

Use diagrams such as on the next page to show what happens when your child puts his money into a bank, ie, you 'lend' it to the bank in exchange for a little bit of interest. The bank in turn lends your money (along with lots of other people's money) to people who wish to purchase something such as a house, car or business etc. They charge these people a higher interest than they are giving you and so this is how they make their money.

Have a look on the internet and compare interest rates that banks are paying against interest they are charging. Mention also that the difference is not all profit, as banks also have to pay wages, rent, insurance and other running costs.

You work hard and save your money

You put your money into the bank and they pay you 7% interest.

BANK
SILBO

The bank lends or invests your money along with other people's money and gets a higher interest rate than it is paying you. This is how banks and finance companies make their money (profit).

The bank invests your money in shares and gets 12% return.

The bank lends your money along with other people's money, to people who want to buy a house. The bank charges them 9% interest.

People use their credit card to buy a TV or meal or stuff. The bank charges them 19% interest on unpaid balances.

Sometimes the lending institutions such as the banks or finance companies make bad decisions. This can result in people losing their hard earned savings. For example: The bank (or finance company) lends all your money and other people's money to someone who has a bad credit rating. They get into difficulties and cannot pay the bank its money back. The bank is then unable to give you your money back and so you have all lost all your savings.

It is important to look into how safe the place is where you want to invest your money. You can do this by checking their credit rating. If you are not sure then it pays to ask advice from professional advisors.

The point of this page is for your child to get the overall concept of what interest is and what the difference between "simple interest" and "compound interest" is.

Apart from saving money so you can use "your own money" instead of paying to use "other people's money", another great reason to save is because the bank (or financial institution) adds interest (a payment made by them to you for the use of your money). There are two types of interest - "simple interest" and "compound interest".

Simple Interest

Simple interest is when you save money and interest is only paid on the original amount put into the account to begin with (called the principal).

Compound Interest

Compound interest is the most powerful. When you're saving, the bank (or financial institution) adds interest to your savings at regular intervals (for example, every month). If you don't touch the interest, but let it add to your lump sum, then you start to earn interest on your interest, as well as on the original amount you saved (an example of passive income).

The following paragraphs on paying interest or receiving interest have been adapted from the book "The Four Laws of Debt Free Prosperity " by Harris and Coonradt.

Paying interest

Interest is an unfair enemy, because he never rests. You become a slave to your lender. You may work 50 or 60 hours a week to keep up with him, but he works 168 hours a week to keep ahead of you. He never takes a lunch or dinner break. He works every Sunday, every holiday, and every night. He has no mercy. He even takes your money when you are sick in bed. If you lose your job and miss too many payments, he will take your house or car or stereo or whatever else you have borrowed for!

Receiving interest

On the other hand interest can become a wonderful friend if you are the lender. Instead of being in the interest trap, interest is working just as hard for you as it used to work against you. Twenty four hours a day, seven days a week, it is earning money for you. It works weekends, holidays, and nights. It never takes a day off, a lunch or dinner break, and it earns just as much for you on the days when you are sick and when you are well, and just as much when you are laying on the beach, fishing etc as when you are working. So therefore when you are receiving interest, instead of paying it, it is the first step to earning "passive income" and becoming financially secure.

How to teach your child this important lesson

Read through this page with your child or have him read and explain what the difference is between simple interest and compound interest.

SIMPLE INTEREST

This is when the bank (or the person you have lent the money to) pays you interest on the amount you have lent them. Each year you get the same amount of interest for your money.

COMPOUND INTEREST

This is when the bank (or the person you have lent the money to) pays you interest on the amount you have lent them. Each month (or year) the interest is added to your amount and then the next lot of interest is worked out on the new total amount.

SIMPLE INTEREST

Year	Principal $	Interest 6%	Total
1	$100.00	$6.00	$106.00
2	$100.00	$6.00	$112.00
3	$100.00	$6.00	$118.00
4	$100.00	$6.00	$124.00
5	$100.00	$6.00	$130.00
TOTAL INTEREST		**$30.00**	**$130.00**

COMPOUND INTEREST

Year	Principal $	Interest 6%	Total
1	$100.00	$6.00	$106.00
2	$106.00	$6.36	$112.36
3	$112.36	$6.74	$119.10
4	$119.10	$7.15	$126.25
5	$126.25	$7.57	$133.82
TOTAL INTEREST		**$33.82**	**$133.82**

What type of interest would you rather choose?

Simple **or** **Compound**

Circle your answer

Compound of course!

- **Use the rule of 72 to show you the power of compound interest**
- **The higher the rate of return the faster your money doubles**

The rule of 72 is an easy rule you can use to work out how your savings or investments can grow with compound interest and how long the investment will take to double. (source www.sorted.org.nz).

Just divide the interest rate (or average annual return) into 72. The result tells you how long it will take for your money to double without further savings.

It needs to be easy to try and work out how fast your money will grow, so using the rule of 72 as a tool is an easy way to do it.

How to teach your child this important lesson

Use the following example to explain the Rule of 72.

For example, if you have $100, which is earning 6% interest (after tax). 72 divided by 6 = 12. That means every 12 years your $100 will double, so:

After 12 years you have $200

After 24 years you have $400

After 36 years you have $800

Also explain that if the amount they had was $1000.00 at the same interest rate as above then the amounts saved would be $2000, $4000 and $8000.

To be completely accurate, you would need to deduct something from the interest rate if you wanted to allow for inflation. For example, if you allowed for 2% inflation, the real interest rate would be 4%.

THE RULE OF 72

is an easy rule you can use to work out how long it will take to

Double your money

Just divide the interest rate (or average annual return) into 72. The result tells you how long it will take for your money to double without further savings.

For example, if you have $100, which is earning 6% interest (after tax).

72 divided by 6 = 12. This means every 12 years your $100 will double,

After 12 years you will have $200

After another 12 years it will have doubled again so you will have $400

After another 12 years it will have doubled again so you will have $800

How long will it take to double my $100.00 if my interest rate is

6%	*will double in 12 years*
8%	____________________
9%	____________________
10%	____________________
15%	____________________

What will my $100 @ 9% be worth in 24 years?

Ask an Adult what interest rate they are getting for their money.

Use the rule of 72 to remind yourself of the power of compound interest.

Answers: 9yrs, 8yrs, 7.2yrs, 4.8yrs, $800

Silbo says

- **Use compound interest to start building long term financial prosperity**

A small percentage increase in the interest rate can make a huge difference as to how much money you make at the end of that investment.

Many people when looking at the interest rate an investment is paying, forget to look at how often the interest is added to the principal. Compound interest that is added monthly is a better investment than Compound interest which is added once per year. Seeing how different interest rates affect the end result of an investment or loan will help motivate your child to find the best investment or loan rate possible. These two charts illustrate why it's important to research how much interest you are getting on any investment (or paying on a loan.)

How to teach your child this important lesson

With both you and your child looking at the chart, have your child pick an interest rate. Choose how many years they want to invest for and then multiply the result of $1 by $1,000 and then $10,000 and finally $100,000.

For example,

$1 at 9% over 40 years grows to $31.41

$1,000 at 9% over 40 years grows to $31,409

$10,000 at 9% over 40 years grows to $314,094

Now do the same with a different interest rate.

Now look at the second graph and see how the same amount increases when the interest is added monthly instead of annually.

Ask your child which they would prefer. Interest added annually or monthly.

These two charts show how $1.00 grows over a period of time.

Graph one the compound interest is added annually. Graph two the interest is added monthly.

Graph one shows $1.00 invested with compound interest added ANNUALLY

Years	3%	5%	7%	9%	11%	15%
1	1.03	1.05	1.07	1.09	1.11	1.15
5	1.16	1.28	1.40	1.54	1.69	2.01
10	1.34	1.63	1.97	2.37	2.64	4.05
15	1.56	2.08	2.76	3.64	4.78	8.14
20	1.81	2.65	3.87	5.60	8.06	16.37
25	2.09	3.39	5.43	8.62	13.59	32.92
30	2.43	4.32	7.61	13.27	22.89	66.21
35	2.81	5.52	10.68	20.41	38.57	133.18
40	3.26	7.04	14.97	31.41	65.00	267.86
45	3.78	8.99	21.00	48.33	109.56	538.77
50	4.38	11.46	29.46	74.36	184.56	1083.66

Graph two shows $1.00 invested but with compound interest added MONTHLY

Years	3%	5%	7%	9%	11%	15%
1	1.03	1.05	1.07	1.09	1.11	1.15
5	1.16	1.28	1.42	1.57	1.73	2.11
10	1.35	1.65	2.01	2.45	2.99	4.44
15	1.57	2.11	2.85	3.84	5.17	9.36
20	1.82	2.71	4.04	6.01	8.94	19.72
25	2.12	3.48	5.73	9.41	15.45	41.54
30	2.46	4.47	8.12	14.73	26.71	87.54
35	2.85	5.73	11.51	23.06	46.18	184.46
40	3.32	7.36	16.31	36.11	79.83	388.70
45	3.85	9.44	23.12	56.54	138.03	819.06
50	4.47	12.12	32.78	88.52	238.64	1725.91

THE DIFFERENCE IS $642.25 MORE, for no extra outlay.

The more frequent your interest is added and the higher the interest rate, the quicker your money will grow.

- **Research how often interest is added to your investments**

History has shown that houses increase substantially over a ten year period, so generally speaking a house is a good thing to get a loan for. However, it is important to understand the different types of loans you can have for a house mortgage and also the "for" and "against" of those loans.

It's important to understand how interest is figured on each type of loan so you can understand how much of your payment is being applied to principal (the actual sum you borrowed) and how much is being applied to interest (what you are paying for the use of that money).

How to teach your child this important lesson

Go through each type of mortgage and explore the differences between each loan. Discuss how when most loans are being repaid that most of the amount is being paid towards interest. The following examples of the different types of mortgages are taken directly from the website: www.sorted.org.nz . Then search the internet for calculators that will show you in a visual form the difference when you pay extra amounts off your loan and how much of a saving you will make in the long term, www.sorted.org.nz also has lots of different calculators.

Types of mortgages

When you're choosing a home loan, there are two big decisions you need to make:

- Whether to take a fixed interest rate, a floating rate, or a mix of both.
- How you want to make repayments: through a table mortgage, revolving credit mortgage, reducing mortgage or an interest-only loan.

Fixed interest rate loans

The interest rate you pay is fixed for a period from six months to five years. At the end of the term, a fixed interest loan automatically moves to a floating rate unless you negotiate another fixed term.

Capped rates are a variation where the interest rate cannot rise, but will drop if floating rates drop below the capped rate.

Floating rate (sometimes called variable rate)

Lenders of floating rate loans will lift or lower the interest rate as interest rates in the wider market change. This means your repayments may go up or down.

A mix of both

It is possible to split a loan between fixed and floating rates. This lets you make extra repayments without charge on the floating rate portion while you get lower rates on the fixed portion.

How you split your loan is important and can be worked out by considering the total extra cash you're likely to get from work bonuses or the like over the period you've set the fixed rate for. This is the amount you could put on a floating rate.

When the fixed rate part of your loan comes up for renewal, if you've paid off some or all of the floating part, you'll need to repeat the exercise for the next year or two.

WAYS OF MAKING REPAYMENTS

Table loan

This is the most common type of home loan. You can choose a term up to 30 years with most lenders. Most of your early repayments go to pay interest, while most of the later payments go to pay off the principal (the lump sum you borrowed). You can take a table loan with a fixed rate of interest or a floating rate.

Application fees for table loans range from nothing to over $1,000. Most lenders which do have a fee, charge around $200 to $400. This is often negotiable.

Revolving credit loan (sometimes called line of credit)

Revolving credit loans work like a large overdraft. Your pay goes straight into the account. Bills are paid out of the account only when they are due. By keeping the loan as low as you can at any time, you pay less interest because lenders calculate interest daily.

You can make lump sum repayments and re-draw money up to your limit. Some revolving credit mortgages gradually reduce the credit limit to help you pay off the mortgage.

Application fees on revolving credit home loans can be up to $500. There can be a fee for the day-to-day banking transactions you do through the account.

Reducing loan

Reducing or straight line mortgages repay the same amount of principal with each repayment, but a reducing amount of interest each time. These are relatively rare in New Zealand. Payments start high, but reduce (in a straight line) over time. Fees are similar to table loans.

Interest-only

You don't repay the money you've borrowed until an agreed time. Some borrowers take an interest-only loan for a year or two and then switch to a table loan; the normal table loan application fees apply.

WHAT DO YOU THINK THESE TERMS MEAN?

Fixed interest ______________________________

Floating Rate ______________________________

Table Loan ______________________________

Revolving Credit ______________________________

Reducing Loan ______________________________

Interest Only ______________________________

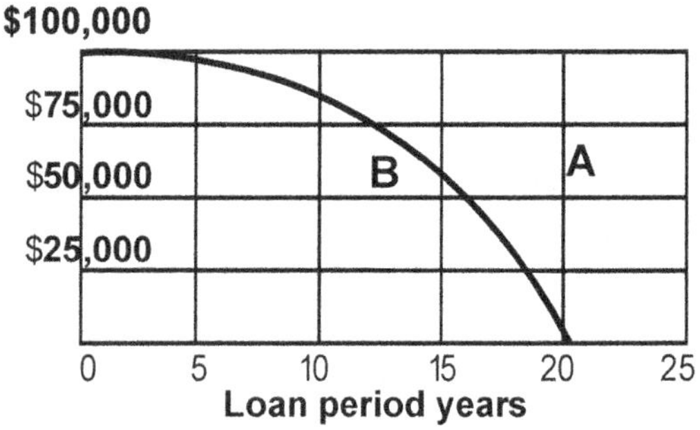

This graph shows a $100,000 loan that would normally be for 25 years (A) but by paying an extra $20 per fortnight the loan will be paid off after 21 years 6 months. (B) Saving 3 years 6 months of payments and a huge $21,036.29 of interest.

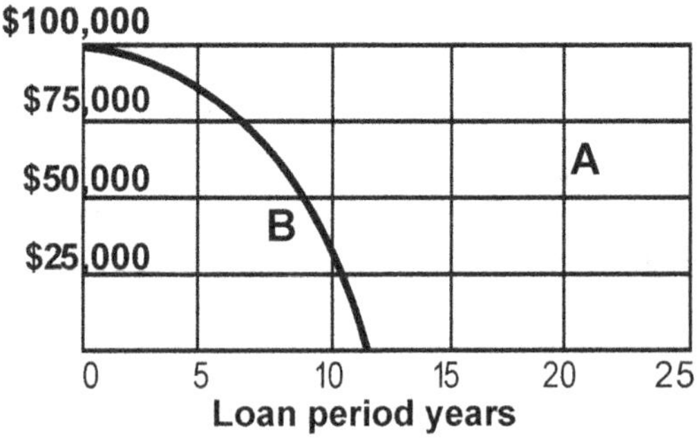

This graph shows a $100,000 loan that would normally be for 25 years (A) but by paying an extra $100 per fortnight the loan will be paid off after 10 years 2 months. (B) Saving 14 years 8 months of payments and a massive $80,565.26 in interest.

Paying your loans off as soon as you can will save you money!

- **Using "other people's money" comes with a cost**

There are two ways to buy things: Using your own money or using other people's money. When using other people's money to buy something, it still has to be paid back using your own money later on with interest added. Many adults do not actually think about just whose money they are spending. Many children do not have any idea where the money actually comes from.

Many children see their parents and other adults getting money from the EFTPOS machine or paying with their credit card. It is therefore hard for them to understand whose money is being spent. It is important to teach your children the difference between using an EFTPOS card (using your own money) and using the banks money (other people's money) as with a credit card. The bank will charge you interest on any unpaid portion of the monthly balance whereas hopefully you are getting good interest from allowing the bank to use your money.

How to teach your child this important lesson

Using the list on the next page, go over the ways you commonly pay for things as an adult and emphasize "your money", "other people's money"

Explain to your child that sometimes even when an adult pays cash for something, if that cash has been obtained from an account that is a credit card or has an overdraft, they are using other people's money. The bank will charge them interest and therefore it will cost them more in the long run.

It may be a good idea for a while to go to the bank (or ATM) and withdraw cash for your purchases such as groceries so your child can actually see cash being spent, and when it is all gone, it is all gone. Be prepared to put some items back if you go over the spending you have allowed. This too can be a great lesson for children and yourselves!

There are two ways of buying things

Using your own money	Using other people's money
Cash	Credit card
Automatic teller machines	Finance company loan
Debit card	Hire purchase
Eftpos	Lay by
Internet banking	Overdrawn bank account (unarranged)
Telephone banking	Bank overdraft (arranged)
Cheques	Bank loan
Automatic payments	Loan from a friend or relative
Direct debits	

Note: The above are using your money when that account has money in it otherwise you are using *other people's money*.

Note: Interest is charged by the person lending you the money.

Using other people's money comes with a cost.

If you can't pay for it fully today

DON'T BUY IT!!

- **Cheques are nearly a thing of the past**
- **Some people will only accept a bank cheque**
- **A cheque is a way to pay for something using your own money**

Cheques are another way for you to pay for things using your own money. When you go to a shop and write out a cheque you are agreeing that you can afford to purchase the item.

If you do not have enough money in your account (insufficient funds) your payment will be dishonoured by the bank. This is commonly called a "bounced" cheque. Your bank will charge you a fee (called a dishonour fee) for the work it takes them to tell the person who accepted the cheque that there was not enough money in your bank account. The person who you wrote the cheque out to can also charge you a fee too. The fee can be around $20.00 or $30.00.

In the past writing a cheque to pay for things was the most common form of payment (apart from cash). However, because many people wrote out cheques when they knew they did not have enough money in their account to pay, businesses stopped accepting cheques because of the risks involved. The Eftpos card has largely replaced cheques. If there is not enough money in that persons account to pay for their purchase then the transaction is "declined" (by the bank) immediately which protects the business. Some businesses will only accept a "bank cheque" as payment. A person goes into the bank and asks the bank for one of their cheques. The bank will write out a cheque to whom and for how much the customer wants them to. The customer pays the bank the amount of the cheque and a fee for the bank writing out the cheque for them. Because the cheque comes from the bank (and the customer has already paid the amount to the bank for the cheque) many businesses are happy to accept a "bank cheque".

How to teach your child this important lesson

Explain to your child what a cheque is. Go through the steps necessary to write out a cheque, explaining the various parts, name and address, date, who the cheque is for, the amount of money the cheque is for, and the signature. Then get a bill you need to pay and use the blank cheque to practice writing out a cheque. If you still use a cheque book to pay for bills, get your child to help you pay your bills. Model a good example to him by filling in the cheque butt!

Explain that the numbers at the bottom of the cheque have the cheque number and the bank number and the branch printed on them. Just the same as discussed in step five on the deposit slip and bank statement.

Here is a sample cheque for you look at and see what they are like.

DATE: 25.04.08
Payee
Stones
Engineering
Item
New Trailer
$ 2,475.17
00521

SILBO BANK
Box 23, Sunny View Rd, Auckland

DATE: 25.04.08

Pay Stones Engineering

The sum of Two Thousand Four Hundred and Seventy Five Dollars and seventeen cents

$ 2,475.17

Account Payee Only

SJ Sample

00521 06 3455 440362: 00

This cheque has been made out to Stones Engineering for the sum of $2,475.17. It has been stamped with Account Payee only, which means it cannot be cashed but must be paid into "Stones Engineering" account only. The numbers on the bottom tell us that it is cheque number is 521, then the other numbers tell us the bank and which branch and then the bank account the money is to come from.

The portion on the left is the stub that is left after you have torn out the cheque. It is your record of who you paid, when, why and how much.

Now you have a turn. Give your child the latest power or phone account and have him pretend to pay them by filling in this pretend cheque.

DATE:
Payee
Item
$
00521

SILBO BANK
Box 23, Sunny View Rd, Auckland

DATE:

Pay Or bearer

The sum of

$

Account Payee Only

Steven and Joan Sample

00521 06 3455 440362: 00

- **Assets keep you financially well**
- **Liabilities keep you financially sick**

Assets and Liabilities are how we measure a person's financial situation and are an indication of how financially well that person is. The more liabilities you have the worse off you become financially and the opposite to that is the more assets you own (not owe money on) the better your financial position becomes.

It's important to understand what assets and liabilities are and how assets are the key to creating financial freedom. An asset is a useful or valuable person or thing. In accounting terms, it's an item that can be converted into cash such as bank deposits, shares or property. In his book, Rich Dad Poor Dad Robert Kiyosaki states that an asset is only something that produces a cash flow. He basically says that if the house that you live in doesn't produce an income then that it is a liability. However, banks and accountants view this differently. Your education can also be viewed as an asset. It has both monetary (fancy word for money) and non-monetary value. Its monetary value is in the increased earnings you expect to get as a result of being a qualified person.

How to teach your child this important lesson

Have your child read the definition of an asset and a liability. If he doesn't include himself as an asset, make sure you tell him he is definitely one. Ask him if he can name some different assets and liabilities. For this exercise use the definition that only something that is actually producing a positive cash flow is an asset.

Look at the Definition of Assets and Liabilities

Assets:

Something that earns you money: Stocks, real estate, business, car (if used for a business to earn a living), gold, silver, coins and rare collectibles.

Liabilities:

Something that costs you money: cars, unnecessary clothes, junk, trinkets, boats (pleasure), stereos, games, sports equipment and computers etc.

Look round your house and see how many assets and liabilities you can see and name. For this exercise use the definition that only something that is actually producing a positive cash flow is an asset.

Assets	Liabilities

Debt is an amount of money, a service, or an item of property that is owed to somebody. When someone loans you money you are indebted to that person. Another way of saying this is that you become a slave to the person or organisation who has lent you the money.

Debt isn't always dumb, because if taking it on MAKES you money in the end it is a very smart thing. When you handle wisely what you have been given, then it is much more likely you will be given more money to handle in the future. The way you determine if taking on debt is smart or dumb is to ask yourself four questions:

1) Is it most likely to appreciate (go up) in value in the future?
2) Will it most likely depreciate (go down) in value in the future?
3) Have I asked someone who is an excellent money manager their opinion before taking on this debt?
4) Who is making payments?

Silbo says a car can be a tricky one when deciding whether it is a smart or dumb debt. Silbo says that if a car is needed (not wanted) to get to a job or used for your job to earn money, then a car is not a dumb debt. However, Silbo says that the purchase of a car becomes a dumb debt when more is borrowed than absolutely necessary and at a high interest rate because of a desire to impress other people. A quote adapted from the Automobile Association website says "You shouldn't over-extend yourself to buy an asset that depreciates as much as a car does. Borrowing for a new car is a costly luxury because of massive depreciation."

Because there's a difference between smart debt and dumb debt, it's important to be able to tell which is which. One buys assets that usually make you money, the other buys liabilities that usually cost you money.

How to teach your child this important lesson

Get your child to think of some things you could buy. Then get him to "qualify" them by asking the four questions above about each purchase. Talk to your child about the different debts you have now and whether or not they are considered smart debt or dumb debt. If you have some dumb debt, explain to your child what your strategy is for getting out of debt. In Step 7 – there is a method called "a debt elimination" programme.

Don't feel bad if you suddenly realise you have made dumb decisions in the past. That does not mean you are dumb – it just means you made dumb decisions with the best knowledge you had at the time. Remember also that we sometimes teach best what we need to learn for ourselves. Teach your children this important lesson so they don't make the same mistakes.

Adverts for encouraging you to take on dumb debt convey the feeling that you are sitting, in a wonderful warm pool, which feels great, so relaxing, so peaceful, and that you will feel fantastic. Nothing could be further from the truth because all of a sudden you realise you are in a swamp full of leeches who are sucking the life blood out of you. The sooner you get rid of one leech, another one clings to you. Unless you take drastic action to get rid of those blood suckers once and for all, you will be stuck with them your whole adult life. Just as leeches get bigger and bigger by sucking more blood, so will your debts get bigger and bigger unless you do something about them.

SMART DEBT

List some things that you consider could be "smart debt."

____

____

____

____

____

DUMB DEBT

List some things that you consider could be "dumb debt."

____

____

____

____

____

If it's not going to make you money and you have to borrow money to get it, think really carefully.

Do you need it??

- **Read contracts when borrowing money and make sure you understand them**
- **Beware of clever salespeople**

Many people do not understand how much their car has really cost them when taking out a car loan. They do not also understand what they are signing. If they take out a loan for a car at 21% percent the car has cost them around double the sale price by the time they pay it back.

Many people are persuaded by a 'slick sales pitch' to buy a particular car, with the line "it will only cost you xyz per week". Sales people are taught to have an answer to overcome each objection the purchaser may have. For example a person who says they can't afford the car because they can't afford to insure it, is told that they can obtain finance for that too. They can just add it to the cost of the loan and pay it in one easy payment. Budget advice services are full of people who have taken out a loan for a car only to find that it causes them significant hardship to pay it back. Many of these people do not understand the "real cost" that their car will cost them in the end when taking out the loan. They also do not understand that their credit rating will be affected in the future if they cannot pay their loan.

How to teach your child this important lesson

Go over the example on the next page with your child and get him to decide whether it is a "dumb debt" or a "smart debt". This particular example is a **real life example** with **exact costs** taken from a finance agreement form. In the example, the person has an old car worth $2000 which is used as a trade in for the new car. Notice that things like booking fee *(the agents fee for doing the paperwork),* comprehensive insurance (compulsory when taking out finance), payment insurance *(to protect the finance company against you not making the repayments)* and mechanical breakdown insurance *(an optional but not essential extra)* have been added to the cost of the car. Interest is then calculated for the whole amount over the four years it takes to pay it off.

If your child really wants a brand new car, do this exercise with him: Give him a small piece of paper and tell him to write $6000 on it and spend a good five minutes decorating it. When he is finished, tell him to rip it up and ignore his protests. This is to illustrate that as soon as you drive a new car out of a car yard, it depreciates $6,000 (more or less) because it is now used. The time he spent decorating the piece of paper represents the time it would have taken him to lose the $6,000.

Let's look at this example of someone buying a car with finance

Car advertised for sale	$7,990.00
Payment insurance	$405.00
Mechanical breakdown Insurance	$760.00
Statutory fees *(Govt fees)*	$3.00
Comprehensive insurance	$995.00
Cost of car	$10,153.00
Less Trade-in	$2,000.00
Amount needed to borrow	$8,153.00

Now Lets Look at what it is going to cost to borrow to buy the car at 19% interest over 4 years

Booking fee	$350.00
Interest charged on total amount ($8153 + $350)	$4,135.46
TOTAL COST TO PURCHASE CAR ($8153+$350+$4135.46)	**$12,638.46**

In other words, he started with a car worth $2000 *(used for the trade-in)*. After four years of paying $263.30 per month (total of $12,638.46) he now has a car that is worth $3000 if he was to try and sell it second hand.

What do you think?

Was this a Smart debt or Dumb debt?

- **Understand how credit cards work**
- **If you can't pay for it fully today, don't buy it**

If you actually have the money in the bank to pay for your purchase, then using a credit card can be a wise use of your money. This only applies when you pay off the balance of your credit card in full by the due date! You can arrange with your bank to have the outstanding balance automatically debited (taken out) of your account so you do not have to pay any interest. The money you would have used to pay for purchases can continue to sit in your savings account, or other investments, earning interest until you need it. Apart from a base fee charged on some cards, you'll incur no other costs.

With things like mortgages and fixed term loans people know that if they make this payment for this amount of time, the debt will be paid off in a certain amount of time, but with credit cards it is a real unknown.

How to teach your child this important lesson

Pretend that you are going to buy a TV set and put it on your credit card. Discuss how you have different options of how to pay for it (the smartest one being to pay it all off by the due date). Go through the example on the page over and discuss how much a TV set would actually cost in the end if someone paid only the minimum monthly payment on a credit card. This was worked out from the website www.csgnetwork.com/credcardmincalc. If you have a credit card, or a "store" credit card, get out the statements and go through it. Show your child where to look for items such as "outstanding balance" "Minimum payment required", "interest rate" etc. Check out websites for New Zealand credit cards. Check for hidden things such as extra fees. On one card there was a charge of $15.00 each three months if you did not use the card.

www.interest.co.nz is another good website to look at for a comparison of different rates of interest rates being charged on credit cards. www.money.howstuffworks.com/credit-card, explains things such as what do the numbers mean, how does the magnetic strip work etc. It may have some items which are peculiar to the American market; however it is still an informative site for a child to look at: www.cscce.com is a website committed to student credit card education.

Pretend you want to buy a new TV for $1,000.00 and you decide to put it on your credit card.

When you get the bill, you have two choices,

1. Pay it off completely with money you have in your savings account.
2. Just pay the minimum payment until it is paid off so you have more money is your pocket to spend now!

Which do you think would be the best?

If you decided to go with option 2 then think about this...

Original cost of TV is $1,000.

If you make the minimum monthly payment of $20.00 per month and were charged 18.5% interest per year.

You would end up paying **$2931.00** for the TV, **PLUS** it would take you **19.25 years!!!!** to pay it off.

Even if you made double the payments it would still cost you $1275.00 and take you 2 years 8 months to pay it off.

How much extra did you pay for your TV when you made only the minimum payments?

$__________

What do you think this TV would be worth in 5 years time if you tried to sell it?

$__________

Answers: $1931.00 . $500.00 if you were lucky.

- **Putting things on credit for short term gain can turn into long term pain**
- **Protect your credit rating**
- **Don't go guarantor for others**

If you are unable to pay your debt, then the debt is often referred to a debt collection agency. The debt collection agency passes this information on to a company who specialises in holding information on peoples past credit history. When you request credit from a store or finance company that store or company then contacts this information company to find out what sort of credit risk you are. Some people don't realise that even when goods have been repossessed and sold to help offset debts owing, that the person who took out the loan originally is still liable to pay the outstanding balance even when they may not have the goods any more. Even an unpaid parking fine that has gone through the above process could affect your ability to buy a home for the next 5 years.

Businesses will go broke if they lend to people who cannot pay their debts. This particular company in New Zealand keeps information on you for 7 years if you have been bankrupt and for 5 years if you have not paid your debts on time. People who have a poor credit rating have to pay a higher interest rate for a loan, because they are a bigger risk to the finance company.

How to teach your child this important lesson

Have your child follow the trail of how a bad credit rating can affect your future. You can also go to www.mycreditfile.co.nz and download a form that you then post in so you can request for free (as long as you are prepared to wait 10 days) what is held on your credit history. Discuss the findings with your child.

The stories Silbo has been told are so sad. It is not uncommon for a person not to be able to afford a payment for a car, or the car needs repairs a few months after purchasing it. They can't afford to get the car fixed and pay the car at the same time. They don't pay the car payment, and so the car is repossessed. The finance company repossesses the car and sells it for whatever they can get for it and then credits the loan account with that amount. Many times because the interest has been added on to the whole loan, the people owe just as much after the car has been taken away, than they did when they had it. They still owe the debt for the car and have to continue paying it even though now they have no car.

Do not go guarantor or put a loan in your name to help someone purchase something on credit. You could become a slave to your lender as they are lending you money (because your name and signature is on the document) and you are the one who will have to pay it back even though your friend or partner may have the goods, or have had them repossessed.

Follow the trail of how a bad credit rating can affect you.

You buy a car on hire purchase but can't make repayments, so the car is repossessed by the finance company. You now have a bad credit rating and your details are held by a credit check company for at least 5 years.

If things turn really bad and you are declared bankrupt, it will take 7 years before your bad record is wiped!!

When you want to buy a house you may find the bank won't lend you money because you had a bad credit rating.

If you want to borrow for a business later on you may find you can't get credit or they want to charge you a much higher interest rate because of your past bad credit rating.

PROTECT YOUR C __________ R __________

If you go guarantor for your friend to get something on hire purchase, and your friend can't pay the repayments you could also end up with a bad credit rating through no fault of your own.

- **Use a debit card instead of a credit card**
- **If you can't pay for it fully today, don't buy it**

New Zealanders spend $1.14 of every dollar they get. (Department of statistics April 2008). How is this possible? Many people get a credit card because in our modern way of life it has become an "essential" for buying over the internet, booking flights, booking tickets for concerts, reserving hotels etc, without having to have cash on you or having to send a cheque. Many people do not realise that there is such a thing as a "debit card" which can be used to buy things on the internet, book flights, hotels etc, but you are using your own money. As soon as the purchase is done, the money comes directly out of your own bank account. The bank usually charges you a reasonable monthly fee for this.

For a short time people can actually spend more than they earn. They can only do this by using credit cards and getting loans to buy things they can't afford to pay cash for. Buying things on credit has become so easy, and because New Zealanders in general seem to have developed an inability to practice the concept of delayed gratification, people find themselves in serious debt very quickly. They find themselves so deep in debt that the only solution has been to file for bankruptcy. Teach kids to avoid credit cards especially when doing tertiary study and use debit cards instead. If they learn to spend and save according to a well thought-out spending and savings plan, you give them an important advantage after they leave tertiary study.

The advantage of having a debit card instead of a credit card is that it tends to protect you from over spending, because when your account is empty and you try to put a purchase on your card it will come up "declined". This could help protect you from making poor financial decisions today with will affect you in the future.

How to teach your child this important lesson

Go through the example on the next page and discuss the differences. If you have a debit card and a credit card show them both and talk about them when you use them.

Look at the Debit card compared to a Credit card

DEBIT CARD	CREDIT CARD
The money comes out of your own account	The money comes out of the bank and you pay interest on outstanding balances
Can't overdraw your account and incur interest charges	You can end up with huge debt and pay high interest
Can use it to purchase goods same as a credit card	Can use it to purchase goods same as debit card
Convenient to use	Convenient to use
Accepted most countries	Accepted most countries

If you can't pay for it fully today,
Don't buy it!

Silbo says

- **Stay away from pre-determined credit and store cards**

Some pre determined credit loans which operate as a "revolving credit loan" also have the ability to have interest free deals added to them as well. Many people think that taking on an interest free loan is fantastic as it gives them plenty of time to pay it off before it incurs interest. They don't stop to think that the retailers wouldn't be doing it if they didn't think they would make money out of it. On some accounts of this type, when payments are made by direct debit, the amount is allocated evenly between each item that still has a balance owing on it. One case I know of worked out that if the person continued with their same payment by direct debit it would take 8 years to pay off a pair of shoes worth $15.10!

Here' is how it worked. On her store credit account she had put different items ranging from a pair of shoes purchased for $15.10, baby clothing purchased for $44.00 through to some furniture at $1677.90 interest free for 12 months. Her overall outstanding balance of her account was around $2,400.00. She was paying $20.00 per week by what the company called "easy pay". What I expected to see was because she had paid $20.00 that week that the shoes she had put on the account for $15.10 were paid off and the next smallest bill would have had the remainder of that payment added to it and so reduced what she owed for the baby clothing. However what was happening was a percentage of her payment of $20.00 was divided over everything she owed. The shoes she had bought for $15.10 were having a payment of 11 cents made to them each time she made a payment and she was being charged 19.90% per annum interest for those shoes as well. The information "behind the scenes" on her account showed that the shoes she had purchased in March 2008 would not be paid off until March 2016 – that is 8 years after she bought them. So, if you have an account like this and are paying by direct debit, check that it is not going to take you 8 years to pay off that pair of shoes worth $15.10 (or whatever it is you have purchased).

How to teach your child this important lesson

Read through and discuss with your child the advertisement on the next page which has been taken word for word from a website. The company's name has been changed to "xyz". Notice how it only tells you the good things and they point out all things that will appeal to a customer. Then read the second advertisement how a spending and savings planner would read the advertisement. Show your child any documents you may have with this type of loan and discuss with him how they work. If you are not sure yourself, take your child to the shop and get someone to explain it to both of you.

Read this advertisement taken word for word from a company website.

"Xyz have a convenient way to shop. Easy and quick. The xyz customer card is a predetermined credit limit that gives you the ease of shopping in our store. Simple to sign up for and only takes a few minutes of your time. Once done you are away to shop freely at your leisure. Making a purchase takes only a few minutes. No waiting around for approval! No more going from point A to point B to sign documents. Paying your account is now even easier! Only 3% of the total has to be paid each month or you can set the amount to pay above that 3%. That's easy. Know your limit. Xyz easy-read statements help you to control your payments and control your purchasing. The other great thing about Xyz is the FREE underground parking! No meter maids to worry about. Have fun shopping with Xyz!"

Now look at how Silbo would interpret the same advertisement!

"Xyz have a convenient way to shop. Easy and quick (to get into debt). The xyz customer card is a predetermined credit limit that gives you the ease of shopping (and spending money you don't have) in our store. Simple to sign up for and only takes a few minutes of your time (because we don't get you to read and understand the fine print so it takes even less time to owe us heaps). Once done you are away to shop freely at your leisure (for wants not needs and book up a big bill so we can charge you around 23% interest when the interest free period ends). Making a purchase takes only a few minutes (to get you into debt which can takes years to repay). No waiting around for approval! No more going from point A to point B to sign documents (just swipe your card and spend some more). Paying your account is now even easier! Only 3% of the total has to be paid each month (so you can spend the next 10 years paying for that pair of shoes) or you can set the amount to pay above that 3%. (which we hope you won't because we will make less money from the interest on your outstanding balances). That's easy. Know your limit (how much you can get into debt). Xyz easy-read statements help you to control your payments and control your purchasing (or spend until you are so far in debt it will take years to pay it off). The other great thing about Xyz is the FREE underground parking! (Woop dee doo) No meter maids to worry about. Have fun shopping with Xyz!" (we look forward to taking your money and making you a modern day slave to your lender).

False Prosperity is having lots of "stuff" that you still owe money on.

Silbo says

- **It's never too early to start saving**
- **Invest wisely**

Those that start saving and investing from an early age have an advantage over those that start later in life thanks to the effect of compound interest.

The longer the time frame that you can have your money invested then the more money you will have when it comes to retirement. This is simply because the effect of compound interest has had longer to work.

How to teach your child this important lesson

Show your child the two different scenarios focusing on the total invested for each and how much was accumulated.

Sue and Sam start to save hard when they are 19 and put $50 a week for 8 years into an investment earning 7% interest.

Age	Save	year end
19	2600	2,600.00
20	2600	5,758.74
21	2600	8,943.85
22	2600	12,351.92
23	2600	15,998.56
24	2600	19,900.45
25	2600	24,075.49
26	2600	28,542.77
27	-	30,540.76
28	-	32,678.62
29	-	34,966.12
30	-	37,413.75
31	-	40,032.71
32	-	42,835.00
33	-	45,833.45
34	-	49,041.79
35	-	52,474.72
36	-	56,147.95
37	-	60,078.31
38	-	64,283.79
39	-	68,783.65
40	-	73,598.51

Jess and Jim spend up for 8 years then save $50 a week for the next 14 years. They also average 7% interest.

Age	Save	year end
19		-
20		-
21		-
22		-
23		-
24		-
25		-
26		-
27	2600	2,600.00
28	2600	5,758.74
29	2600	8,943.85
30	2600	12,351.92
31	2600	15,998.56
32	2600	19,900.45
33	2600	24,075.49
34	2600	28,542.77
35	2600	33,322.76
36	2600	38,437.36
37	2600	43,909.97
38	2600	49,765.67
39	2600	56,031.27
40	2600	62,735.46

By the time Sue and Sam are 40, they will have **contributed $20,800** **for a total of $73,598.51**	By the time Jess and Jim are 40, they will have **contributed $36,400** **for a total of $62,735.45**

Ask your child which one they would prefer.

Ask him what the most significant difference is between the two scenarios and let him know the biggest advantage he has over any adult is **TIME!**

When do YOU think you should start saving? NOW!!!!

No taxes or inflation have been included as the point of this exercise is to show how much better off you are when you start saving early

Again, share your own investing experiences with your child if you have any.

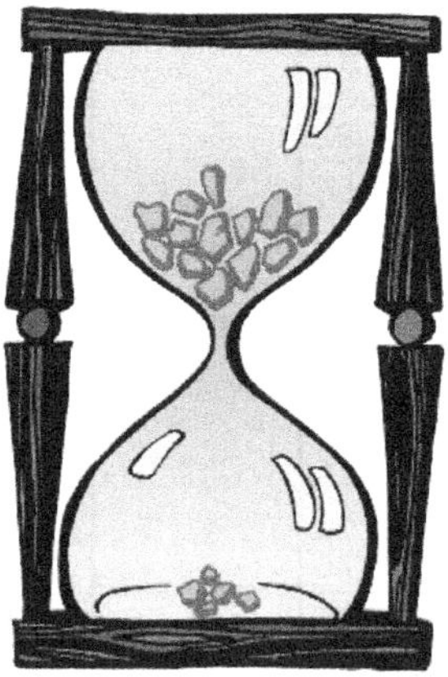

It's never too early or too late to start saving.

- **Don't put off saving until tomorrow**

Saving from an early age is the most important factor to becoming financially well in the future.

It is the compound effect of interest on top of your savings that will give you the financial freedom you want for your early retirement. This is excluding any profits made from business investments, property, stocks and shares etc.

How to teach your child this important lesson

Using the chart below, look at how much has to be put away each week in order for there to be a million dollars when your child retires. Show your child how as time goes by and the later they leave it to start saving, then the more has to be put aside each week to get the same result.

If you haven't done so already, talk to your child about your investment strategies and how they have developed over the years. Did you start saving early enough?

Time is on your side so start saving now!

If you want to have $1,000,000 at retirement, look what you must save every week, depending on your age when you start with a 9% return.

Years to retirement		Savings per week
40	$	54.49
35	$$$	85.35
30	$$$$	135.07
25	$$$$$$	217.35
20	$$$$$$$$	359.81
15	$$$$$$$$$	626.87
10	$$$$$$$$$$	1211.04
5	$$$$$$$$$$$	3071.11

Be kind to yourself. Start saving now!!

Taxes have not been taken into consideration with these calculations

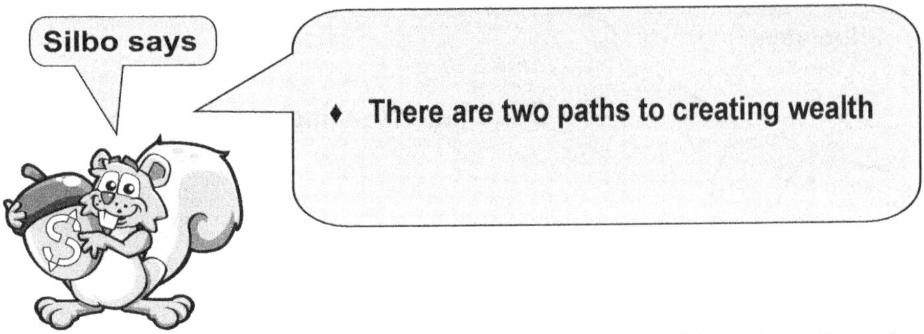

Our money can work for us in two ways. By doing something where the value of what you are doing appreciates or by doing something that generates regular passive income or cash flow. Appreciation of assets and passive income can both be generated from the same source but just in different ways. The source of this wealth can come from stock, shares, real estate or business and depending how you use them is how you will get your money working for you.

As discussed in earlier steps, passive income is the fastest way to creating financial freedom. Once you have enough passive income to cover all your outgoings, then you have the freedom to do whatever you fancy with your time or other money. Using the two paths to creating wealth gives you the opportunity to diversify your strategy for wealth creation. You can decide to go down the path of investing in shares or stocks, buying and selling real estate or perhaps buying a business that will increase in value. This method will give you wealth through the assets increasing in value and hopefully you will sell them for much more than you paid for them. Alternatively, you may buy stocks or shares, which will give you regular dividends, real estate from which you will receive rental income or perhaps a business that generates good profits and you no longer need to work in it.

How to teach your child this important lesson

Have your child look at the two paths to creating wealth and look at how wealth can be generated in different ways. Talk about diversification so you don't have all your financial eggs (all the fruits of your labour) in one basket. No matter which of these ways is used, they can all lead to financial freedom if done with getting the correct advice from the right people and being aware of all the facts.

As an added activity, you could have your child search the papers or internet and look for items that talk about financial success stories and where people have created wealth through different means.

Your money can make you money in two ways using the

Two Paths to Creating Wealth.

APPRECIATION

When your assets or investments increase in value and you can sell them for more than you paid for them.

PASSIVE INCOME

When your assets or investments create an income that you don't have to work for.

Real Estate

Stocks

Business

- **Learn to evaluate advantages and disadvantages of different types of assets**

Different types of assets can have different advantages depending on your own situation. Often it can depend on timing in your life as to what assets you own.

When we look at the different types of assets that are available, we can see that timing or our own lifestyle could affect the decision whether it would be to our advantage or disadvantage to purchase now, later or not at all.

How to teach your child this important lesson

Have your child look at the different assets and help them think about the advantages and disadvantages of each type.

Cash

Advantage	Disadvantage
____________	____________
____________	____________

Gold

Advantage	Disadvantage
____________	____________
____________	____________

Jewels

Advantage	Disadvantage
____________	____________
____________	____________

Forestry

Advantage		Disadvantage
______________		______________
______________		______________

Livestock

Advantage		Disadvantage
______________		______________
______________		______________

Real Estate

Advantage		Disadvantage
______________		______________
______________		______________

Ideas

Advantage		Disadvantage
______________		______________
______________		______________

- **Know what the return is you are getting on your investment**

It is important to know what the "return on your investment" (ROI) is. This is also known as "rate of return" and refers to how much your money is earning for you. ROI is used to compare returns on investments where the money invested is not easily compared using a dollar amount. Instead it is shown as a percentage. The higher the percentage, the higher the return.

Once your child is ready to start investing their money, it is important they know what investments are making the best return for the amount invested. By understanding what the ROI on an investment is, your child will get to know where to put their money to get it working hardest for them.

How to teach your child this important lesson

Look at the example of the two items and compare the monetary return against the return on investment. If you had $1000 to invest, which one has the best return on investment (ROI)?

Return on Investment (ROI)

If you bought a new camera for $1000 and then sold it for $1200.

Monetary return would be $200.

ROI (Return on investment) would be 20% ($200 divided by $1000).

If you bought a new cell phone for $100 and then sold it for $140.

Monetary return would be $40.

ROI (Return on investment) would be 40% ($40 divided by $100).

***Answer**: If you had $1000 to invest, then you would be best to buy 10 cell phones at $100 each and sell them all for $140 each to make a profit of $400 (because the cell phones have a higher return on your investment).*

- **Don't put all your fruits of your labour in one basket**

With investing, there is a direct link to Risk vs Return. It is a case of "the higher the risk, the higher the return (or loss)". It is therefore important that investments are spread over a number of different assets such as stocks, bonds, real estate, gold and others. This is called diversification and reduces the risk of losing everything should things go wrong. When you have a number of different investments, this is called an investment portfolio.

Teach your child to look at the different investment opportunities and to share their investment money between two or three different types of investment. This will reduce the risk of losing all of their money if for some reason it does not perform well or actually goes broke and they lose their money. It is better to only lose a little than to lose the lot.

How to teach your child this important lesson

Talk about the risks involved with having all your fruit in one basket and the potential to lose the lot. Have a look at the newspaper or listen to the news and talk about the many big companies that are having financial difficulties and how many people have lost their life's savings recently because they had all their money with one investment type or company.

For example if your investments were all in airport shares and the airport had to close due to an earthquake destroying the runway, then the shares would drop in value and you could lose everything you invested.

> **"Insanity is doing the same thing over and over again, but expecting different results."** **Rita Mae Brown**

RISK VS RETURN – DIVERSIFICATION IS THE KEY

Think about these assets and decide how you would invest $1000 of your savings.

Do you think it would be smart to have: (circle which one you think)

All Cash **Yes/No** 

All Gold **Yes/No** 

All Livestock **Yes/No** 

All Forestry **Yes/No** 

All Jewellery **Yes/No** 

All Real estate **Yes/No** 

How would you like to invest your money?

$_____+ $_____+ $_____+$_____+ $_____+ $_____ =$1000.00

No one likes to lose money. Make sure you do your research before making the investment

Diversification is the key

- **Pay tax on each and every dollar you earn**
- **Taxes contribute to the running of our community**

Tax is money which individuals and organisations must pay to the Government, as required by law. For people who are employed, it is taken out of the money they're paid by their employer to do their job. For people who are self employed they must keep records of how much they earn and pay tax themselves direct to the Government. When someone is self employed they can deduct some legitimate expenses from their income (such as mileage for their car when it is used for their business) which reduces the amount of tax they need to pay.

Using New Zealand as an example, the government uses the money to benefit the New Zealand community to pay for important public services like roads, welfare, healthcare and education, including paying people like teachers, nurses and doctors and providing help for people who are unemployed. If people don't pay tax when they should then there is less money available that the Government can use for the provision of these services. Every New Zealander pays some tax from the time they spend their first pocket money at a shop as there is a tax called GST (goods and service tax) which is calculated and paid to the Government for most things. Wages are exempt from GST. Other countries have GST or VAT

How to teach your child this important lesson

Look at the pie chart Core Crown Expenses with your child (used with permission from the NZ Treasury Department). The Treasury Department (Crown) spends the money it collects on taxes and from other revenue (income) areas. Ask your child what services he and his family have used that the Government has paid for to instil in him the importance of paying taxes. Then look at the pie chart Core Crown Revenue that explains where the government collects its revenue from. Look at the website *http://www.whatstax.govt.nz/* to learn about when you need to start paying tax and more information on why we need to pay tax. Talk about where most of the money comes in from and where it goes out to.

Research other nations to see how other countries receive and spend taxes. You may be surprised to find out that some countries do not help people when they are out of work.

Example of how tax money is used in New Zealand

Core Crown Expenses in 2007/08 – $56.1 billion

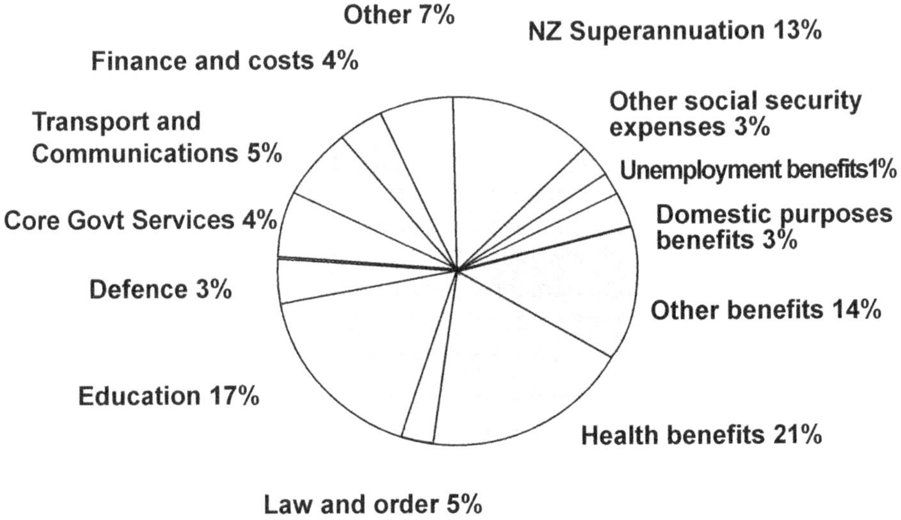

Core Crown Revenue in 2007/08 – $59.4 billion

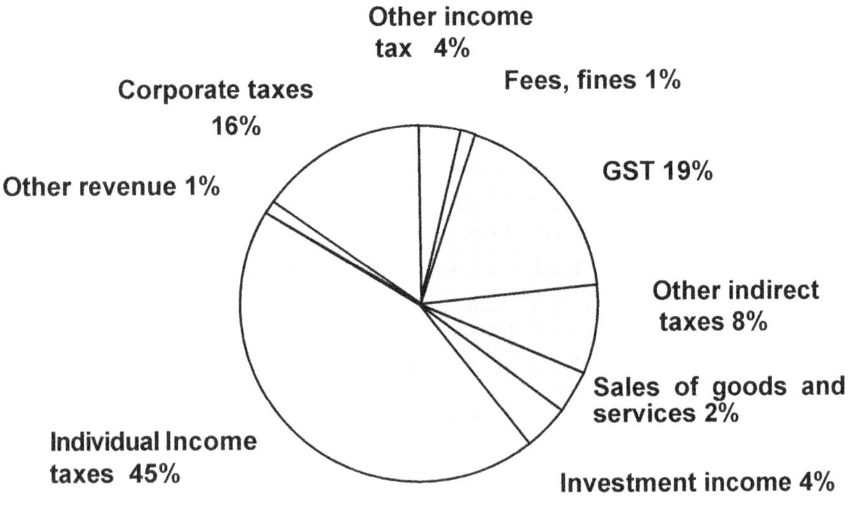

Graphs used with the permission of the New Zealand Treasury

Source. http://www.treasury.govt.nz/budget/2007/taxpayers/02.htm

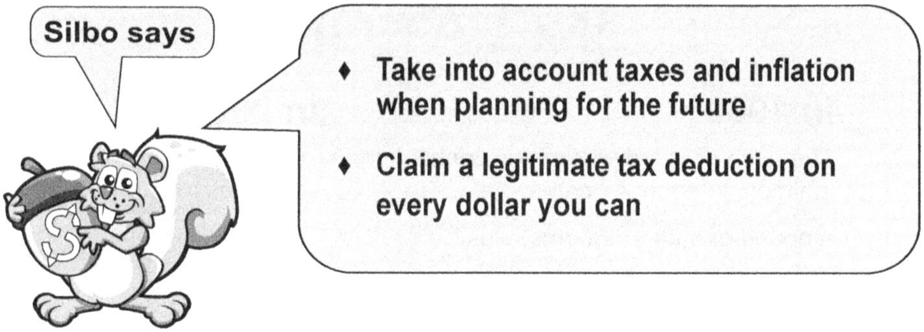

Taxes and inflation are two things that happen that we don't have a lot of control over. However, when people do not claim back tax that they are legitimately allowed to do then they are wasting dollars that can be put to work to earn them money for the future. Inflation means that the cost of things goes up over time so it is important to allow for it to minimise the impact it will have on your savings in the future.

It is important to pay what tax you owe. However, it is just as important to understand the tax laws so that you can legitimately claim any tax deductions off your income to minimise the amount of tax you pay. From a savings point of view, the effects of taxation and inflation mean that you may not have as much money in the future as you thought you would. You may also find that the money you have at retirement does not buy as much as it does now. The New Zealand Government has a target of keeping inflation at under 3%. The small difference in the interest rate can make a huge amount of difference over a long period of time. Letting large sums of money sit in a savings account that makes less than 3% interest actually COSTS the saver money. Learning to evaluate investments and move your money to earn a higher rate of interest as soon as possible is critical when working toward financial prosperity.

How to teach your child this important lesson

Use the examples over the page to show the effects of inflation and taxation. Contact different banks and financial institutions and find out what the minimum balance you need is in an account to start earning a higher rate of interest. This is so inflation doesn't eat up the interest you earn. Show your child a supermarket docket, petrol docket etc and they will see GST (goods and service tax) added at the end. Explain to him that he will start paying tax as soon as he spends the first bit of money given to him.

Have a look into various organisations that advertise that their donations are tax deductible. Talk to your child about organisations that you support (or could support). If you have a donations rebate form you could show your child how this works. If you haven't in the past collected receipts for donations you have made to tax deductible charities then it is important to do this as you are missing out on a tax refund.

INFLATION

In 1960	In 2008
The price of bread was seven pence halfpenny (approx 7 cents).	$2.50
A pound of butter (500gms) was Two shillings (approx 20 cents)	$3.90
A dozen eggs cost four shillings and four pence (approx 44 cents)	$3.80
A quart of milk (1 litre) cost eight pence (approx 7 cents)	$2.00

Inflation is when you pay $11.00 to go the movies when it used to cost you $7.00

TAXES

Work hard and earn $100.00 but then **take off (approx) 20% tax and you are left with $80.00**

Buy something for $100 and **add Goods and Service Tax of 12.5% and it now costs you $112.50**

Earn $100 interest on your savings account. Then you **pay tax of 33% (depending on your income level) and you are now left with $67.00**

Taxation is what you give the Government before you give to yourself.

We at Silbo Systems trust you have gained a lot of valuable information from reading this book. The money and life skills taught here are nothing new and have been around for hundreds of years. But, unless you go out and practice what you learn, the information soon gets lost or forgotten.

We hope that **you** will go out and practice what you have learned. We also hope that you will then pass the skills on to your children and grandchildren so that they are ready and prepared to cope with everything that life throws their way.

If you have a great story of how these lessons have helped you, then we would love to hear from you and to share them to encourage others.

If you would like to get our newsletter or to find out when and where our next lessons will be, then contact us via our website.

Sylvia and the team at Silbo Systems.

info@silbo.co.nz

www.silbo.co.nz

64 27 631 8524

New Zealand

Also available in the Silbo Systems collection

Money Lessons for Life - Children's activity workbook.

This A4 size workbook has all the lesson activities that are used in the book "Parents How to stop your kids going broke". It is also designed as the workbook to match the "Money Lessons for Life Parents Resource Book". In both situations it is ideally suited for the child/student to do the activities as you work through the lessons.

Money Lessons for Life - Parent Resource Manual

This A4 size resource manual has the same content as "Parents How to stop your kids going broke". It is set out in a user friendly A4 bound manual format suited to a teaching situation. It takes you through all eight lessons in a step by step guide and includes the child's activity workbook. If you wish to teach your children essential money and life skills then this manual will give you the tools to do it.

Licensing opportunities

Are you interested in helping people become more financially intelligent?

Contact Silbo Systems to register your interest in becoming a Silbo Systems educator in your community.

Fundraising opportunities

Do you belong to an organisation that needs to fundraise? Silbo Systems can help.

1. Have us come to you as a speaker - sell tickets.
2. Sell "Parents - How to stop your kids going broke".

This book is also available as an E-Book from our website

www.silbo.co.nz

For more information about any of these products and opportunities

Contact info@silbo.co.nz

Made in the USA
Monee, IL
04 November 2026

67385481R00115